CE
SACRAMENTO PUBLIC LIBRARY
3033
D0529399
JAN 30 1985

Central Library
828 I Street
Sacramento, CA 95814-2589

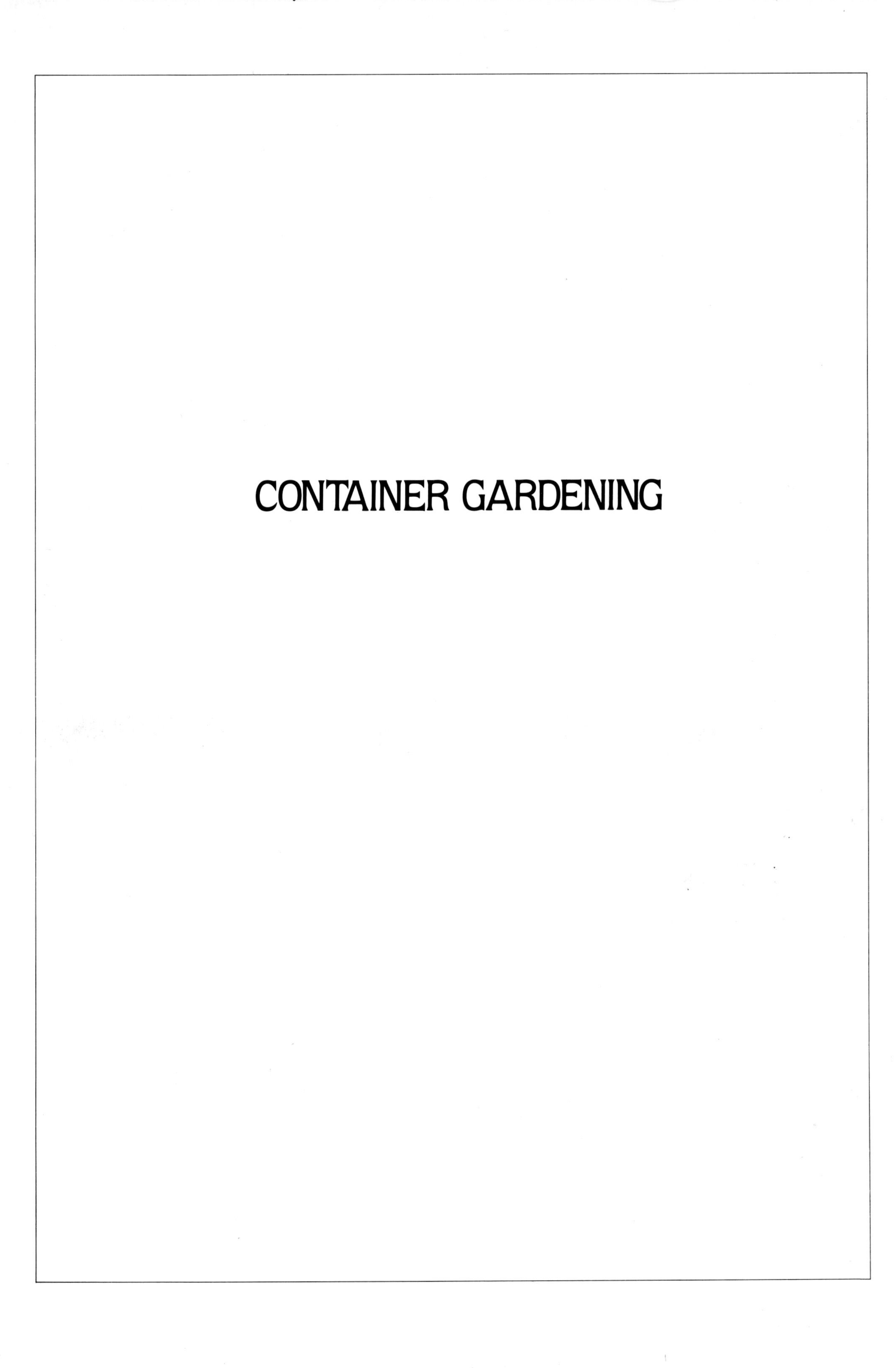

CONTAINER GARDENING

The American Horticultural Society
Illustrated Encyclopedia of Gardening

CONTAINER GARDENING

The American Horticultural Society
Mount Vernon, Virginia

For The American Horticultural Society

President
Dr. Gilbert S. Daniels

Technical Advisory Committee
Everett Conklin
Mary Stuart Maury
Dr. John A. Wott

Container Gardening Staff for The Franklin Library/Ortho Books

Editorial Director
Min S. Yee

Supervisory Editor
Lewis P. Lewis

Editor
Ken Burke

Art Directors
John Williams
Barbara Ziller

Creative Director
Michael Mendelsohn

Contributing Writers
The editorial staff of Ortho Books

Special Consultants
R. J. De Christoforo
Alice H. Quiros

Illustrators
R. J. De Cristoforo
Leavitt Dudley
Ron Hildebrand

Production Director
Robert Laffler

Production Manager
Renee Guilmette

For Ortho Books

Publisher
Robert L. Iacopi

For The Franklin Library

Publisher
Joseph Sloves

The cover photograph shows a small but colorful container garden on a redwood deck. The garden includes salmon-colored crossandras, yellow marigolds and gazanias, red and pink impatiens, white Reiger begonias, purple streptocarpus, and lavender exacum, with English ivy trailing at the base of each container. Consultants, Michael George Vasillopulos and Miho Shinbo. Photograph by Clara Aich.

Contributing Photographers
William Aplin
Martha S. Baker
John Blaustein
Ernest Braun
Clyde Childress
Tyler Childress
Ken Garrett
Fred Kaplan
Michael Landis
Elvin McDonald
Michael McKinley
William R. Reasons
Paul Thomas
Tom Tracy

Additional Photography
Ann Ashley

California Redwood Association, San Francisco, California

Don Chambliss, Director, Home of Guiding Hands

J. W. Courter, University of Illinois

Charles Marden Fitch

George C. Ball Co.

Gulf State Paper Company

Duane Hatch, Oregon State University

Ron Hildebrand

Scott McGilvray

James K. McNair

Colin McRae

William C. Mulligan

Burt O'Neal

Muriel Orans

Ortho Photo Library

Pan American Seed Company

Joseph Parker

Paul Ecke Poinsettias

Redwood Domes, Aptos, California

Rogers Nursery, Costa Mesa, California

Sequoia Nursery, Visalia, California

Michael West

Produced under the authorization of The American Horticultural Society by The Franklin Library and Ortho Books.

Copyright ©1974, 1975, 1976, 1977, 1979, 1980 by Ortho Books. Special contents ©1981 by The American Horticultural Society. All rights reserved under International and Pan-American Copyright Conventions.

Every effort has been made at the time of publication to guarantee the accuracy of the names and addresses of information sources and suppliers and in the technical data contained. However, the subscriber should check for his own assurance and must be responsible for selection and use of suppliers and supplies, plant materials, and chemical products.

No portion of this book may be reproduced in any form or by any means without permission first being requested and obtained in writing from The American Horticultural Society, c/o The Franklin Library, Franklin Center, Pennsylvania 19091. Portions of this volume previously appeared in the Ortho Books *House Plants Indoors/Outdoors, Container and Hanging Gardens, The Facts of Light About Indoor Gardening, Wood Projects for the Garden, Gardening with Color, All About Fertilizers, Soils & Water, Award-Winning Small-Space Gardens, All About Vegetables, All About Growing Fruits & Berries, Gardening Shortcuts,* and *The World of Herbs & Spices.*

Library of Congress Catalog Card Number 81-67191
Printed in the United States of America
12 11 10 9 8 7 6 5 4 3

A Special Message from The American Horticultural Society

Container gardening is gardening at its most versatile. Anyone can do it, from a city dweller with just a windowsill to a suburban home owner with a patio or deck to a farming family with unlimited space but little leisure time. And the variety of plants that can be grown in containers seems endless. Flowers, fruits, vegetables, foliage plants, even shrubs and trees are available to suit all needs, all climates, all locations, all seasons. Container gardening is, in fact, an all-purpose concept in gardening.

Mobility and adaptability are two of the many advantages of container gardening. The approach of winter need not affect you if you are a container gardener. Simply move the plants inside or to a more protected location. You don't have to wait for spring to enjoy daffodils. Learn how to force them early indoors. A large garden is not necessary for growing zucchini. Grow them vertically on a trellis anchored in a container. You don't need a strawberry patch to grow fresh strawberries. They flourish in containers.

Container Gardening is filled with information and advice about growing and caring for plants in containers. Its sections will tell you what kind of soil to use, how often to fertilize, what pests and diseases to look out for, what to do when you go away on vacation, and which varieties of what plants are better for growing in containers. A chapter is devoted to hanging baskets and those plants that are particularly suited to growing in them—good practical information for people who have limited surface space. A chapter on bonsai introduces that fascinating and specialized form of container culture that was begun several thousand years ago in China. Another chapter even gives detailed instructions on how to make different kinds of containers.

Container Gardening will broaden the gardening horizon of the houseplant enthusiast, give confidence to the uncertain novice, and add a new dimension to the activities of the experienced gardener. It is a truly practical guide that will be useful to anyone who is interested in gardening.

Gilbert S. Daniels
President

CONTENTS

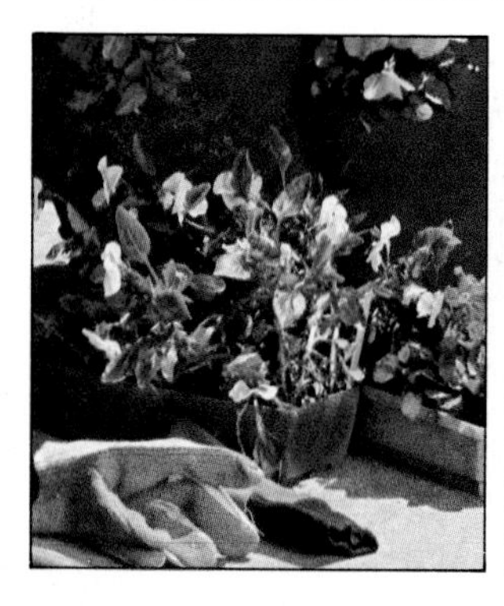
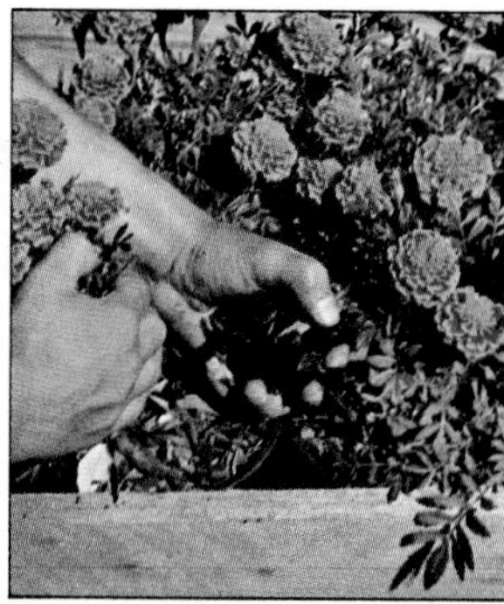
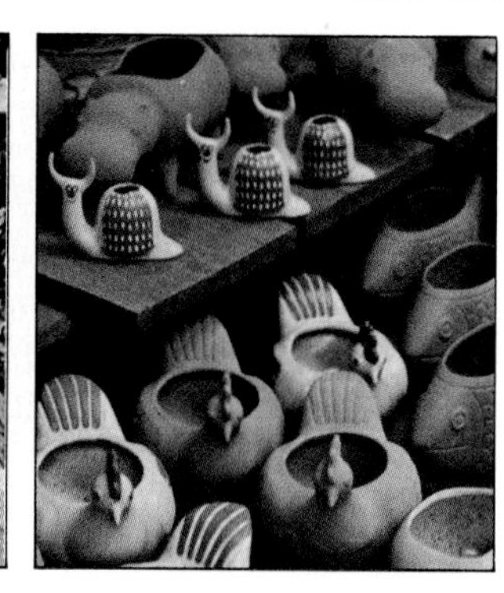

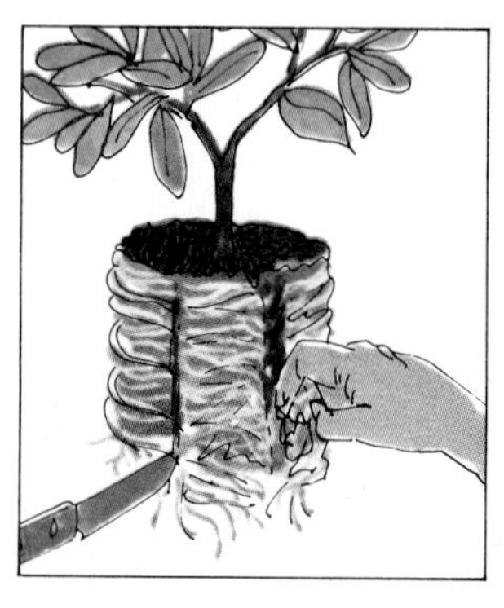
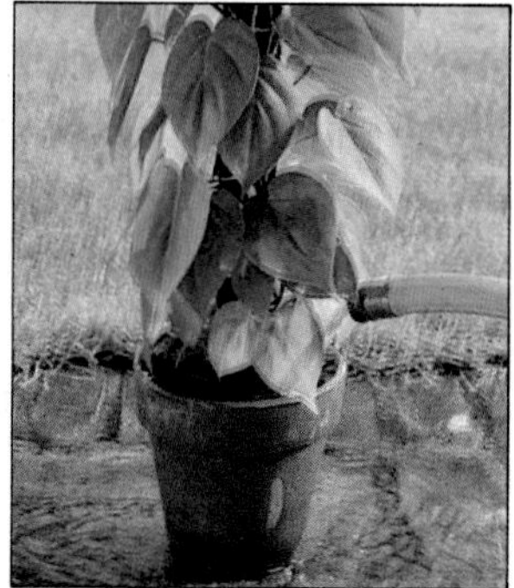
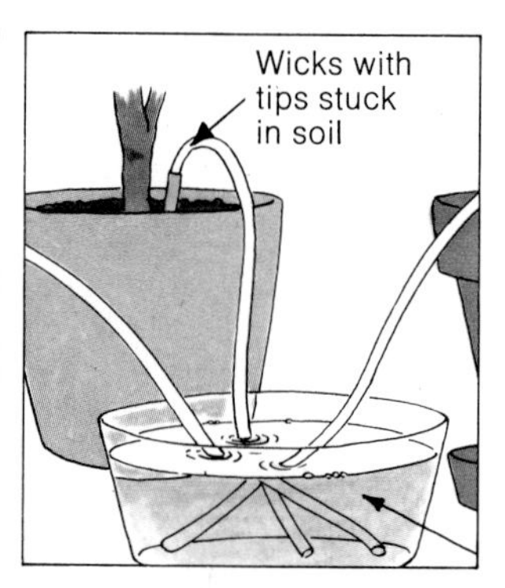
Wicks with
tips stuck
in soil

Hanging Baskets 38

Even if you don't have any surface space at all for growing plants you can still have a garden by using hanging baskets. This chapter tells you how to make a hanging basket, illustrates different types of hanging containers, and lists several plants whose growth habits make them look particularly attractive in hanging baskets.

Annuals, Perennials, and Vines 50

This large group of plants has such a wide range of colors, shapes, and cultural requirements that there is something for everyone. The characteristics of over a hundred plants are given in this chapter, with comments about their growth habits, colors available, the exposure and climate in which they do best, and suggestions for the type of container most suitable for them.

Shrubs and Trees in Containers 66

All plants can be grown in containers, but some tolerate container conditions longer than others, so it is better to select slow-growing plants whose growth you can control and discipline more easily. This chapter describes fifty flowering and foliage shrubs and trees that are particularly attractive or suitable for growing in containers.

Forcing bulbs is an easy way to get a head start on spring, and this chaper gives step-by-step directions on how to do it. There is a chart that lists the characteristics of the best bulbs for growing in containers. Other sections detail problems and pests you may encounter so that you can prevent them from arising.

Fruit trees are admirably suited to growing in containers. Because the containers can be brought inside or moved to protected locations, most fruits can be grown outside their native, in-ground environment. And dwarf varieties are a manageable size. Soil, watering, and feeding guidelines are given in this chapter, as well as suggestions for suitable plants.

This is container gardening at its most practical. You can match the growing spot to the vegetable—warm weather vegetables in full sun and cool weather vegetables in partial shade. This chapter gives the growing needs of all the favorite vegetables and recommends varieties and containers. There is also a diagram of two basic small space container gardens.

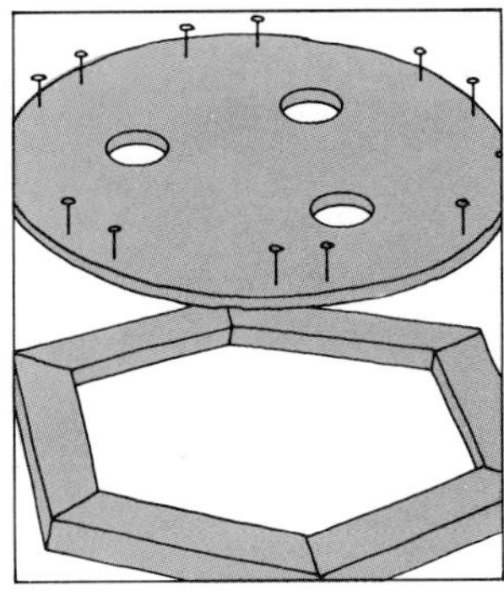

This colorful arrangement of potted primroses was moved here to create a feeling of an early spring garden.

THE VERSATILITY OF CONTAINER GARDENS

Mobility and adaptability are the chief advantages of growing in containers.

This book tells you how to grow plants in all kinds of containers. Container planting is for everyone and anyone who wants plants of some sort close by but doesn't have land to grow them on. Container gardening is the great equalizer, allowing even the urban apartment dweller to plant flowers, fruits, vegetables, vines, shrubs, and trees in just about anything that will hold soil—boxes, bowls, tubs, plastic pails, garbage cans, clay pots, ceramic pots, hanging baskets, hanging bouquets, wire mesh, and even outdoor carpet. There is even information on how to build some of the containers pictured in the book.

This book teaches you how to select plants, when and how to plant them, and how to care for them. It discusses containers in and around apartment houses, townhouses, roof gardens, balconies, decks, and suburban patios. It recognizes that in addition to the dedicated and "total" gardener who is interested in all areas, there are many people who may not care about "gardening" as a hobby but who do enjoy the ambience, color, and companionship that small trees, shrubs, or any of a number of flowering plants bring to the patio, deck, and balcony, and even inside the house or apartment.

Containers and Plants

When you put a plant in a box, tub, or pot, you immediately give it a new character; it stops being a mere bush and becomes an individual shrub with its own distinction.

Often, the simple act of going down to the nursery and looking at the most common plants with an eye to placing them in containers can change your whole idea of how to use plants. For example, when a low-growing juniper is hugging the ground, it's just a ground cover—but when it's elevated in a box, pinched and pruned for a windswept look, it becomes a work of art. Plants seem to have both a garden personality and a container personality. Container gardening is the pleasantest way possible to enter the world of gardening for the first time. With the nursery as your partner, it's difficult to fail. And container gardening may well intrigue you into becoming interested in and perhaps even undertaking more areas of gardening.

The Japanese style. Capturing the spirit of nature—in the forest, the high country, or the seashore—is perhaps easier for the container gardener in miniature than for the landscape gardener on a large scale. A well-placed small rock or two, some moss, and a small piece of driftwood can create a distinct environment that will complement and enhance your choice of container plants. As one such gardener says:

"Our first step toward the Japanese garden came after we bought a hibachi. It looked so dinky—rather silly, really—up near the barbecue area. So we framed a small square in the ground just off the patio and paved it. On this we put two lava rocks (we shopped around for mossy ones) and into it we sank a gallon can of mondo grass. Now the hibachi sits framed as important as you please."

Above: Here the container itself enhances a display of pansies.
Right: Tomatoes, lettuce, onions, and strawberries are all good candidates for containers.

Another gardener relates:

"I planted a cool, shaded mini-forest in a large, shallow container right outside the kitchen window. I began with a dwarfed pine and a groundcover of miniature mint. I surrounded the pine with a feathery club moss and one dwarf fern."

Whether or not you choose to plant in the style of the Japanese, it's worthwhile acknowledging (and making use of) their basic contribution—the setting off of plants, whether singly or in natural groupings. By arranging a stage for a few choice plants in the part of the garden you use most often, you get the greatest effect for the least amount of time, energy, and money.

Mobility. One advantage of container plants is that you can move them.

"As I look around the place now," says one veteran container gardener, "many a plant in a box or a tub carries me back to other homes and other people. That mugho pine in the little cedar box came from the balcony of an apartment house. It was 'loaned' to us to keep until the owners found a proper place for it. Well, I have pinched its candles to keep it small for nine years now, and it looks like it will be around for another nine years. The sago palm in the tub has traveled with us through three changes of address. We bought that dwarf spruce for an indoor Christmas tree about 30 years ago.

"Trees I planted are giving shade to others now—tree houses for children of children. I have planted many gardens. These few boxes, cans, and tubs that have traveled with me are the important plants in my garden today."

The mobility of container plants extends beyond just letting you move your plants from home to home; it also lets you bring in new color almost instantly. You need never have a dull season in your container garden.

The special interest of container plants. When you grow plants in containers, you get to know and appreciate them better than you would if they were grow-

Left: Bulbs can be mixed with other flowering plants to give a longer show. In this case daffodils are combined with primroses. Above: Almost any annual can be used to create a hanging flower arrangement.

ing in beds or borders. This is especially true of a container garden on an apartment balcony, a mobile home terrace, or a small patio.

Because the patio climate is modified for the comfort of humans, it is ideal for some plants but difficult for others. Most plants benefit when shaded from the hot noon-day sun; however, they won't thrive if the morning and afternoon sun are blocked out. In such a case, you'll need to grow shade-tolerant plants—impatiens, fibrous begonias, ferns, and the like.

Plants in containers can be trained into new growth patterns. A clematis that will climb 15 feet or more can be shaped as a 3-foot-wide umbrella above a 12-inch pot. Ivy can follow a curved wire, drape with simple grace, or grow as a formal column. The geranium usually looks like it belongs on a kitchen windowsill, but trained as a standard—a patio tree—it becomes elegant and formal.

Cucumbers grow so fast that watching them form on a hanging vine actually can be a spectator sport. If you don't want a strong vining type in an elevated container, you might try planting one of the bush-type cucumbers—such as 'Patio Pik'—in an 18- to 24-inch box.

The container world. No matter what kind of container you plan to use, make sure you start with a commercial planting mix (see page 22). It will give the plants the aeration (air in the soil) they need for root development. Since the amount of air in the soil is determined by the drainage of water through the soil, good drainage is more crucial for a container plant than for a garden plant. The bottom of the container breaks the blotter (capillary) action of water moving through the soil.

Handling transplants in packs or small pots from nursery to container is easy enough—all the delicate initial nurturing has been done already. And once the seedling or plant is in the container and growing, you can learn whatever you need to know about gardening directly from it.

Shopping in a nursery can be rewarding when you learn how to look for the healthiest plants. These marigolds are for those who want to add immediate color.

The Nearly Instant Garden

Plant suppliers get more "instant" year by year; nurseries offer a shifting rainbow of "instant" color in nursery flats and in 4-inch pots season by season.

How "instant" your plants are depends on you. Gardeners who enjoy growing plants from seed to transplants claim that when you buy plants in flower, you miss most of the fun of gardening—all the sights along the way from sprouting seed to flower.

This may be true, but there are also many good reasons for using the nursery as your greenhouse. When you buy a fibrous begonia in bloom, you have a flower that is 16 weeks from seed. And you save so much growing time with many of the most useful plants: ageratum, 12 weeks; browallia, 12; coleus, 10; geranium, 16; impatiens, 12; lobelia, 12; nierembergia, 12; petunias, 12-15, snapdragons, 14; and thunbergia, 12-16.

The shade problem. Shade offers welcome comfort on a warm summer day, whether it comes from a wide-branching tree, a vine covering a pergola, the roof of a deck, a patio, or an outdoor living room. When a small lot is landscaped for human comfort, using hedges or fences for privacy and wind control, the amount of shaded area increases. As trees grow and increase their spread, they block or filter out more sun.

Consequently, there comes a time in a garden's growth when "full sun" areas are hard to find. That's when you need to start thinking in terms of shade and plant growth. There are many gradations of the word "shade"—dappled sunlight, filtered sun, partial shade, light shade, filtered shade, half shade, shadow shade, and deep shade.

The area next to a patio receives a combination of shade and partial shade. In June it briefly receives the early morning and late afternoon sun. A white wall

Top: Nursery plants in bloom were bought for the display on this deck. The deck is precut lumber, 2" × 4" nailed to 4" × 4". The bark mulch helps keep the area free of weeds.
Right: This partially shaded area, featuring cylinders of impatiens, shows that with proper selection of plants, containers can work in most gardening conditions.

adds reflected light throughout the year. The 3 o'clock sun edges into a portion of the planting. Considering how plants grow and flower in varying degrees of "partial shade," container plants seem to offer a sensible way of managing a patio shade garden. This system lets you move the least shade-tolerant plants to the spot receiving the most light to increase flowering; then, when flowering begins, you can set them back in the shade.

The newer varieties of impatiens are among the best performers in the shade. These excellent container plants will bloom outdoors all summer; then, if you cut them back, you can bring them into the house for winter color.

In thinking about shade, however, you must consider the summer climate of your garden. If cloud cover or fog allows only filtered sunshine, anything less than full exposure is risky. However, if the sun shines almost daily and temperatures climb, many sun plants will welcome some shade.

In addition to shade-tolerant color producers such as ageratum, browallia, begonias (fibrous and tuberous), forget-me-not, fuchsia, lobelia, and nicotiana, there are also shade plants with leaf color that outshines many of the flowering plants. Two examples are the fancy-leafed caladium and coleus.

Coleus. The single-colored and variegated forms of this plant are available in many sizes, leaf forms, and leaf variegations. Plants in the Carefree series are bushy, dwarfed, and well branched, with small narrow leaves 1-1½ inches long. Grown from seed and sold as bedding plants and in pots, they remain bushy in a container outdoors or indoors with a minimum of pinching back.

Research with cutting-grown variegated coleus shows that the leaf color of a plant varies with changes in temperature and day length. In short days and low temperatures, the leaves become narrow and the color is restricted to an area surrounding the midrib. The ideal temperatures for coleus are 70° day temperature and 62° night, with a 16-hour day.

A flower stand built in steps with 2" × 8" risers and 1" × 8" treads.

These steps become a garden grandstand with rows of petunias, marigolds, and ageratum in nursery flats, 4" and 6" pots, and some transplanted into stained clay pots.

Using a quick-change box eliminates transplanting. Either 6" or 1 gallon containers can be used. Bark can be used to adjust the height of the plants and as filler around the tops of the pots.

Container discipline. You learn to really look at plants as you work with them close up in pots, boxes, and tubs. As you deal with plants on more intimate terms, the individual structure and character become important. Not every shrub or tree adapts readily to container growing, but in general those of formal character are easier to handle. For example, the classic sweet bay *(Laurus nobilis)* and the dwarf forms of the Carolina cherry laurel *(Prunus caroliniana)* can be clipped and sheared into all sorts of formal shapes.

Few shrubs benefit more from the discipline of container growing than the oleander. If grown naturally, it often is used as a thick screen or windbreak and grows 10 to 14 feet high—a broad, bulky, multistemmed shrub. Grown as a single-trunked tree in a container, however, its character becomes tailored and handsome. You can choose from many varieties and many colors—there are single flowers and double flowers, ranging in color from white to pink, salmon, and reds. You can shape your container tree to suit by pruning and by pinching out tip growth. Several varieties are available in nursery-trained tree form, including 'Cherry Rips', 'Sealy Pink', and 'Sister Agnes'.

For instant color, you might buy dwarf oleanders in full bloom in gallon cans. If you transfer them to 12-inch pots in August, by September they will look like

This carpenter box holds fifteen square 4" pots of marigolds, moves around with ease, and can be changed when necessary. See plans on page 134 to convert this box into a miniature greenhouse.

Containers can be very ordinary but made quite presentable in the right holder. Here daffodils are planted in the bottoms of plastic bleach containers.

ever-blooming pot bouquets. 'Petite Pink' and 'Petite Salmon' are true dwarfs that were developed by the Los Angeles State and County Arboretum and released to wholesale growers for distribution in the South and California. They rate high as container plants.

Considering all the advantages of growing oleanders in containers, you shouldn't be deterred by these few precautionary measures: (1) *don't eat any part of the plant—all of it is poisonous;* and (2) *keep away from burning leaves and prunings —inhalation of the smoke can cause severe irritation.*

More flowers. The life objective of all plants is to produce seeds. With annuals this must be accomplished in a single growing season. Fading flowers signal the beginning of seed production. At this time, much of the plant's energy is diverted away from the production of new stems, leaves, and flowers and channeled instead into seed formation. To ensure the plant's ability to produce new flowers, remove the fading flowers by pinching or cutting them back at ½ to 1 inch below the old flower head.

If your plant has more seed pods than flowers, don't throw it away. Cut it back, fertilize and water it, and watch it start all over again. Plants such as petunias, snapdragons, and verbena, among others, respond well to this drastic treatment.

Ground covers. Don't overlook the chance to use ground covers in planters underneath shrubs and trees. For example, if you train wisteria as a small tree in a large tub or box, you might dress up the planting with a mulch of ground bark. Or, for a more decorative effect, you might use a ground cover—ajuga for a white wisteria, or evergreen candytuft for a purple wisteria. Beneath container shrubs and trees, you can also plant "living mulches"—Irish moss, Scotch moss, dianthus 'Tiny Rubies', thyme, camomile, arabis, and many other hardy ground covers.

Pillow packs. Ordinary plastic kitchen-type bags—vegetable bags, refrigerator bags, bread bags, or trash bags—are potential pillow packs if they're filled with lightweight synthetic soil. Or you can buy plastic tubes of a specific length at a plastic supply shop.

To make the pillow pack, fill the pillow, bag, tube, or "sausage" with the mix to within 2 or 3 inches of the top. Fold the plastic at each end and sew or staple them closed. Slit the plastic where the seedlings are to be inserted. To make watering easier, insert open-ended small cans (such as frozen juice cans with both ends cut out). Use one or two cans in a small pillow (one can about every 18 inches in a long tube). Provide drainage by punching small holes in the bottom of the pillow. Start a liquid feeding program after the plants have been in about three weeks.

Pillow packs (see text) can be used in sizes to fit many types of containers.

This railing box had plastic pots of daffodils in the spring. They were replaced with blooming petunias, also planted in plastic bottles.

A garden bench built on two large flue tiles brings the plants within easy touch.

The best way to grow flowers and vegetables in the tubes or other sheet-plastic containers is to arrange them next to each other in a nursery flat or shallow box. Expose only the planted portion of the pillow to the sun. Then, when the plants are in flower, you can display the pillow in any fashion you wish—in baskets, for example, or on steps.

Use the nursery all year round. A container gardener can take advantage of the nursery not only in the spring planting season but also in the off-season. Your patio can display a succession of flowers to celebrate the shift of seasons. Mobile containers allow you to plan special seasonal displays. You can establish a "holding ground" in a corner of the garden for containers not on display. This is almost a necessity when container gardening is in high gear, for the holding ground serves as a recovery room for plants, as well as a resting place for containers in their off-season period.

Plants that adapt especially well to container growing include: fuchsias; rhododendrons (both dwarf and deciduous); azaleas; dwarf Japanese maples; the lily-of-the-valley shrub *(Pieris japonica)*; dwarf conifers; slow-growing pines; camellias; dwarf spirea; and oakleaf hydrangea *(H. quercifolia)*.

Current favorites. There are favorites of the season, favorites for hanging bouquets, favorites for containers, favorites for borders, and favorites for edging along a walk. Try the 'Imperial Blue' pansy—an All-America bronze medal winner. Everything the catalogs write about it seems true; it blooms from late winter into the summer. It takes the hot weather wonderfully. The color is a clear light blue, with contrasting bluish-violet faces and a gold eye. Combine the 'Imperial Blue' in hanging bouquets with alyssum 'Tiny Tim', and plant it in wide, shallow containers along with the golden-yellow faceless pansy, 'Golden Champion'.

The Madagascar periwinkle, sold as *Vinca rosea*, more correctly *Catharanthus roseus*, is a summer favorite. This weather-proof plant looks fresh and clean in the hottest weather and stays that way all summer long. As a pot plant it grows to about 10 inches tall and as wide.

The Instant, Portable Water Garden

Carol and Bill Uber, the moving spirits of the Van Ness Water Gardens in Upland, California, grow water plants in containers on terrace balconies, decks, and patios.

You can create a large water garden that delights the eye with its beauty and the ear with its sound of moving water. Or you can work on a smaller scale with a round, portable, 2-foot tub.

You can use a 25-gallon plastic pool, 21 inches wide and 19 inches deep, available from Van Ness Gardens. These containers can be dropped into more decorative half wine-barrels, with heavy casters for greater portability. Grow all the plants in gallon-sized plastic or clay pots and arrange them in the tub at the varying heights needed for each type of plant.

Hardy water lilies. In frost-free areas, you can plant hardy water lilies in February through October. In winter-cold areas, plant them in April to August. Van Ness Water Gardens advises these methods of winter care:

"Hardy lilies may be wintered over safely in the pool if the roots do not freeze. In extremely cold climates, cover with boards and give an extra covering of straw. Should it be advisable to lift the lilies before cold weather arrives, they may be stored in a cool cellar. Be careful that they do not dry out or dry rot will attack them and they will be lost."

Tropical water lilies. Set out the tender, tropical lilies only after nights get warm and stay warm—May 15 to September 30, depending upon your location. Van Ness Water Gardens says:

"In mild climates they may be left in the pool all winter. We do not guarantee them to live over, but almost without exception they do in the mild-winter areas of Southern California. In May, get in and see that the bulb is ½ inch under the soil, and crown (rough) side up. In cold climates, take the bulb out after the lily has gone dormant. Store in a can of moist sand in frost-free cellar or garage until May. Plant. Tropicals have so many blooms and are so beautiful they are worth this little extra work."

About the hardy lilies, Bill Heritage, author of *The Lotus Book of Water Gardening*, says:

"The elegant, almost exotic, beauty of water lilies creates the impression that

Clean water formula

For each square yard of surface area, your water garden should contain:

Oxygenating plants—2 bunches of 6 stems.
Water lily—1 medium to large plant.
Snails—12 ramshorn or trap-door water snails.
Fish—2 fish, 4 to 5 inches long.

A plastic container used as a portable lily pond. The oxygenating plants, seen below the surface, are an aid in keeping the water clear.

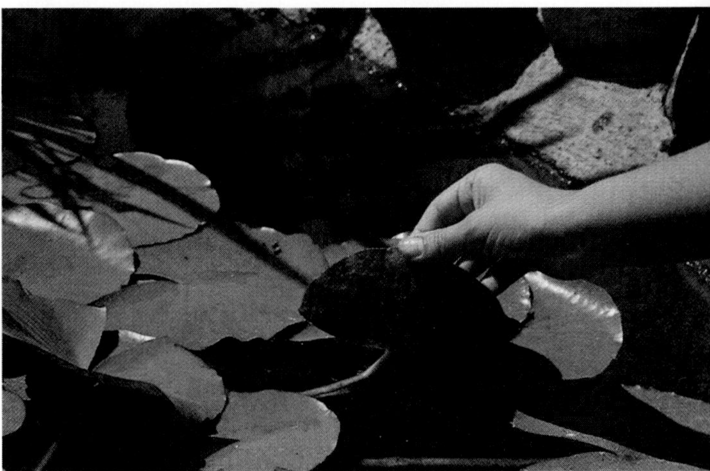

The lily serves the pond in two ways: beauty, of course; and its pads act to hold oxygen. Oxygen bubbles appear on the undersides of the pad.

they must surely need much expertise to grow, and coddling to survive the rigors of winter. In fact they require no winter protection whatever throughout Britain and in most parts of North America. Their constitutions, far from being delicate, are robust enough to survive considerable abuse.

"The hardy water lilies are perennial; growth disappears each autumn and is renewed every spring, year after year. They dislike shade, violent currents, and cold mains or spring water. All they need to flower abundantly summer after summer is correct planting, a comfortable depth of water for the variety and a place in the sun. The more sun you give them the more flowers they'll give you."

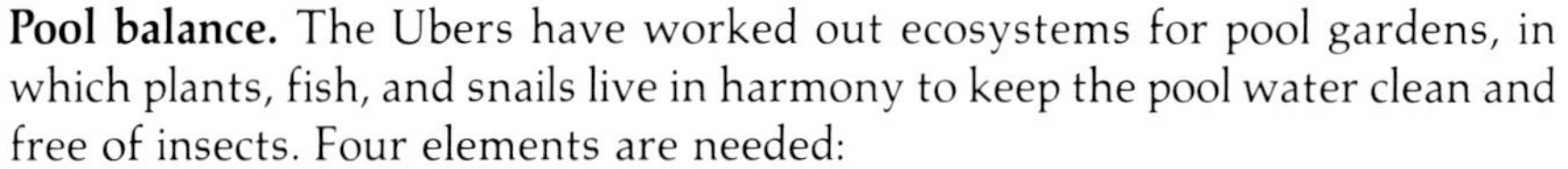

Pool balance. The Ubers have worked out ecosystems for pool gardens, in which plants, fish, and snails live in harmony to keep the pool water clean and free of insects. Four elements are needed:

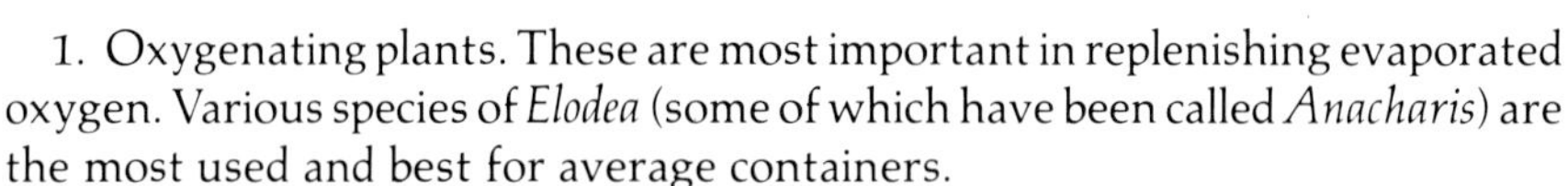

1. Oxygenating plants. These are most important in replenishing evaporated oxygen. Various species of *Elodea* (some of which have been called *Anacharis*) are the most used and best for average containers.
2. Water lilies. These are essential—their pads provide surface coverage, preventing loss of oxygen and keeping the water cooler.
3. Snails. They eat algae, fish wastes, and decaying matter, which otherwise encourages algae growth.
4. Fish. Fish eat such pests as aphids, flies, mosquito larvae, and other insects. (But be aware that overfeeding fish with commercial fish food will change the water balance drastically.)

This tub contains several edible plants. The reed-like stems are water chestnuts; the arrow shaped leaves are violet stemmed taro; the round leaves are lotus; and watercress appears at the right rim.

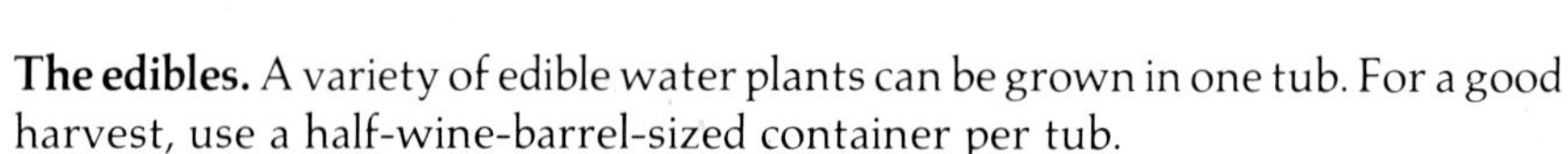

The edibles. A variety of edible water plants can be grown in one tub. For a good harvest, use a half-wine-barrel-sized container per tub.

If you use a 25-gallon container for each type of plant, the size of your harvest will be approximately the following, according to Bill Uber:

"A planting of lotus in April will produce five or six edible roots when harvested during their dormant period in October or November of the second year. The roots of the lotus can be French-fried, like potatoes.

"A tub of 30 to 40 Chinese chestnuts will grow sedgelike, numerous, hollow stems to 2 feet or more, from bulbs in the first year. Then, when they're dormant, you can expect to harvest about 100 chestnuts. A few from the harvest should be saved for a second year planting.

"An early planting of five or six violet-stemmed taro *(Xanthosoma violaceum)* in April will produce arrowhead, 5 to 7 inch, bluish-green leaves on violet stems about 2 feet high, then go dormant about six months later. Harvest during this dormancy will yield enough tubers for about two dishes of poi. (Only the tubers are edible.)

"Watercress gives an almost instant crop."

An Endless Assortment of Pots

This page is devoted to a clear-cut presentation of a shopping guide for plant containers. Here is a look at various container assortments in garden stores; functional plastic waste baskets, buckets and garbage pails at supermarkets; and choice offerings in hardware stores and import shops. Without considering the gadgetry of the hanging basket, there's a big, varied, fascinating collection of containers to choose from. The container you are seeking may be manufactured for nursery plants or an oversize casserole for the kitchen, or whatever. Containers are where you find them. Let your imagination be your guide. And consult the chapter "Containers to Make" (pages 124-141) to learn how to construct your own. Of course, choosing a plant to fit a container is a favorite pastime of its own, and you'll find many pages in this book for guidance.

Whether you're looking for a pot to fit a plant or a plant to fit a pot, here are some of the endless possibilities to choose from.

With proper care these schizanthus and forget-me-nots will stay in bloom for weeks.

CONTAINER BASICS

Container plants have different soil, watering, and cultural requirements than in-ground plants.

A special soil mix is necessary, according to the most successful commercial growers of container plants and according to hundreds of thousands of home gardeners who have bought and used a container mix. Garden stores everywhere sell special container mixes under a wide variety of trade names—Redi-Earth, Jiffy Mix, Metro Mix, Super Soil, Pro-Mix, and many others. However, just because they are known as "soilless mixes" or "synthetic soils" doesn't mean they're artificial. In fact, they contain only natural ingredients.

Basic Ingredients of Container Culture

The organic part of the mix may be peat moss, redwood sawdust, shavings, bark of hardwoods, fir bark, pine bark, or a combination of any two.

The mineral part may be vermiculite, perlite, pumice, builder's sand, granite sand, or a combination of two or three of them. The most commonly used minerals are vermiculite, perlite, and fine sand.

Vermiculite (Terralite). When mined, this resembles mica. Under heat treatment, the mineral flakes expand with air spaces to 20 times their original thickness. Water is retained within the granules of vermiculite.

Perlite (Sponge rock). When mined, this is a granite-like volcanic material. When it is crushed and heat treated (1500°-2000°F.), it pops like popcorn and expands to 20 times its original volume. Unlike vermiculite, the water retention in perlite is around the granules rather than in them; consequently, perlite tends to dry out faster than vermiculite.

Sand. There are many kinds of sand available, but for gardening use, washed and screened quartz sand is superior. The coarser products should be favored for their aerating qualities. Unscreened sand will contain a range of particle sizes and not aerate as well. Sand is commonly used as a component of container soil mixes, for rooting cuttings, and occasionally used in very large quantities to modify the texture of clay soils.

The mix you buy may be 50 percent peat moss and 50 percent vermiculite, or 50 percent ground bark and 50 percent fine sand, or other combinations of the organic and mineral components. The ingredients in the mixes vary, but the principle behind all mixes is the same: soilless "soil" must provide:

1. Fast drainage of water through the "soil."
2. Air in the "soil" after drainage.
3. A reservoir of water in the "soil" after drainage.

Most important in any container mix is the air left in the soil after drainage. Plant roots require air for growth and respiration. In a heavy garden soil, there is little space (pore space) between soil particles. When water is applied to the soil, it drives out air by filling the small pore spaces.

A container mix has small and large pores (micro pores and macro pores). When the mix is irrigated, water is held in the micro pores but quickly drains through the macro pores, allowing air to follow.

Soil Structure

Compacted Soil: The particles are packed close together with little space left for air or water.

Crumbly Soil: Decomposition of organic matter helps aggregate dry particles into porous crumbs.

Saturated Soil: If about half the water from rain or irrigation does not drain through the soil, plants may drown.

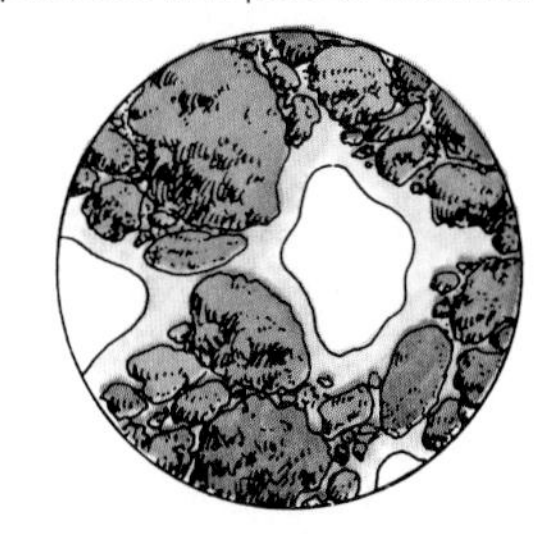

Moist Soil: A film of water between soil particles, and air in all but the small pores, means soil is well drained.

How Does Your Soil Rate in Good Drainage?

The ideal soil is one that holds moisture and at the same time allows a constant flow of air through the soil—bringing oxygen to the roots and removing carbon dioxide from the soil. The ideal soil is a combination of the good points of sand and of clay. Sand provides fast drainage and good aeration, but fails in the water-holding department. Clay is tops in water-holding ability, but dangerously low in supplying air to the soil.

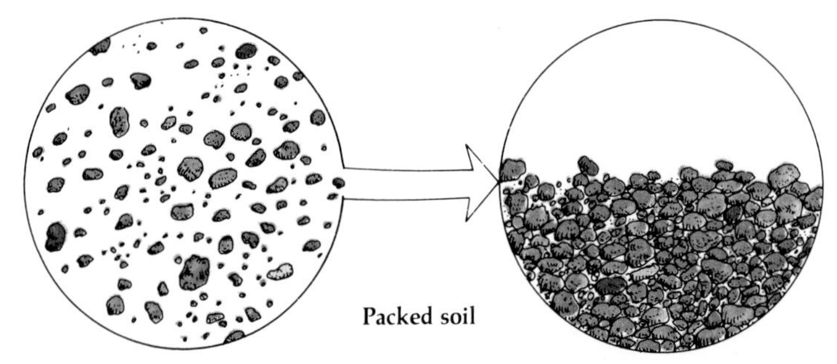

Individual, non-aggregated particles pack into a solid mass with no space for air or water.

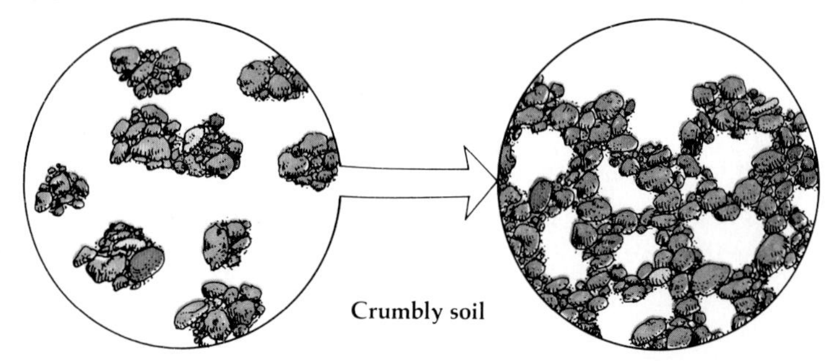

Cultivation and the addition of organic matter aggregate the particles into porous crumbs or granules.

When water fills all the spaces in the soil, air is forced out and plants may drown. In well drained soil there is a film of water and air in each space.

Air space after drainage. Plants vary greatly in aeration requirements (percentage of air space after water from an irrigation has drained away). For example:

Very high—Azaleas, ferns, epiphytic orchids. Many commercial growers of azaleas grow them in straight, coarse peat moss to get this high aeration.

High—African violet, begonias, daphne, foliage plants, gardenia, gloxinia, heathers, terrestrial orchids, podocarpus, rhododendron, and snapdragon.

Intermediate—Camellias, chrysanthemums, gladioli, hydrangeas, lilies, and poinsettia.

Low—Carnations, conifers, geraniums, ivy, palms, roses, stocks, Strelitzia, and grass.

Fir bark

Drainage: Container soil versus garden soil. Many plants will grow in a garden soil where the rate of absorption is as low as ½ inch an hour. Under container growing conditions, however, rates of 5 to 10 inches per hour are considered minimum.

Water moves with continuous capillary action through a column of soil in the garden. A more porous material—gravel or air bubbles—will break that continuity (blotter action), and water will build up wherever the continuity is broken. A drop of water needs another drop of water behind it to drip out of a pot or into a layer of gravel. How much air is left in the soil after drainage is mainly what determines the plant's growth. The percentage of air in soil is less by volume in a 3-inch pot than in a 6-inch pot.

Perlite

Air and water. Take a look at the physical properties of the mixes and the materials that go into them in terms of the following characteristics: fast drainage; reservoir of water; and air after drainage. The figures in the accompanying table indicate percent by volume.

Sand

Material	Total Porosity	Water Retention	Air Space After Drainage
Clay loam	59.6	54.9	4.7
Sphagnum peat moss	84.2	58.8	25.4
Fine sand	44.6	38.7	5.9
Redwood sawdust	77.2	49.3	27.9
Perlite, 1/16–3/16"	77.1	47.3	29.8
Vermiculite, 0–3/16"	80.5	53.0	27.5
Fir bark, 0–1/8"	69.5	38.0	31.5
1:1, fine sand: fir bark	54.6	37.4	15.2
1:1, fine sand: peat moss	56.7	47.3	9.4
1:1, perlite: peat moss	74.9	51.3	23.6

Vermiculite

While water retention doesn't vary a great deal among the above materials, the residual air space does. Without sufficient air around the roots, most plants will suffocate. Water plants will survive in a heavy clay loam but orchids need lots of air, as is provided by fir bark.

If you want to make your own container mix. If you plan to do a lot of container gardening and to use large containers for shrubs and trees, you could make your own mix (according to the formulas that follow), or you could buy a prepared commercial mix. Which one you use depends on what you are going to do with the mix.

Redwood soil conditioner

As a home gardener, you rarely will need large quantities of a mix designed for seedlings and small pots. But when you are growing seedlings or seed in pots, the growing medium must be sterile.

When you only need a few cubic feet of container "soil," a commercial mix is your best bet.

If you'll be using more soil than that, however, you can blend these components together to get 1 cubic yard of very lightweight mix for seedlings and pots:

9 cubic feet of peat moss
9 cubic feet of vermiculite
9 cubic feet of perlite
5 pounds of 5-10-10 fertilizer
5 pounds of ground limestone

Peat moss

For a slightly heavier mix for seedlings and pots, try this:

14 cubic feet of peat moss
7 cubic feet of fine sand
7 cubic feet of perlite
5 pounds of 5-10-10 fertilizer
8 pounds of ground limestone

All these formulas use a fertilizer mix of 5-10-10 instead of combinations of superphosphate, calcium, or potassium nitrate in the amounts called for in the Cornell Bulletin #43 (see page 29). Check the bulletin if you wish to duplicate their procedure in producing the Peat-Lite mixes.

For indoor foliage plants, try this mix.*

14 cubic feet of peat moss
7 cubic feet of vermiculite
7 cubic feet of perlite
5 pounds of 5-10-10 fertilizer
1 pound of iron sulphate
8 pounds of ground limestone

For shrubs and trees, use:

sawdust or ground bark
9 cubic feet of fine sand
18 cubic feet of ground bark or nitrogen-stabilized sawdust

or

9 cubic feet of fine sand
9 cubic feet of peat moss
9 cubic feet of ground bark

To either of the mixes for shrubs and trees, add:

5 pounds of 5-10-10 fertilizer
7 pounds of ground limestone
1 pound of iron sulphate

*If you only need a small quantity of soil mix, but you still want to mix it yourself, a good approximation would be to substitute ½ gallons for cubic feet and ounces for pounds in the formulas given above.

Keep it simple. Some gardeners believe that every type of plant requires a special soil mix and like to work out complicated mixes of five or six ingredients. They just won't accept the fact that a simple combination of peat moss and vermiculite, or perlite, or fine sand, can be used with almost all types of plants, from cacti to tropicals. In that case, however, you do have to modify your watering routine according to the individual plant's needs.

This doesn't mean that you shouldn't tamper with the mix you buy. On the contrary—if the mix is so lightweight that the container will tip over in a slight wind, by all means add sand. Many gardeners, unwilling to leave well enough alone, add garden topsoil to the mix when planting shrubs or trees in containers. But when you add soil you lose all the advantages of a sterilized mix. For example, if you were growing container tomatoes in a soilless mix to avoid soil-borne tomato diseases, it would hardly pay to add garden soil—that would amount to inviting the same diseases you so scrupulously tried to stave off.

The standard soilless mixes are free of disease organisms, weed seeds, and insects. All the nutrients needed for initial plant growth are usually included in the mix. The soilless mixes are ready for immediate use. If you bring home a 2-cubic-foot bag, you will have enough "soil" for 20 to 22 gallon-sized containers, or 35 to 40 pots 6 inches deep. You'll need 4 cubic feet for a planter box 24″ × 36″ × 8″ deep, like those shown on page 99.

The light weight of Jiffy Mix and other peat moss/vermiculite mixes comes in handy when it's time to move containers from one spot to another, or when your "patio" is a roof or balcony, where weight can be a problem. Jiffy Mix weighs less than half as much as garden soil when both are soaked.

1. Begin by gathering all the basic ingredients you'll be using.

2. Measure each ingredient into a separate pile.

3. Start the blending process by combining all the ingredients into a single pile.

4. Rebuild the pile three to five times until all the ingredients are thoroughly distributed.

Homemade mixes. If you want to make your own mix, choose the ingredients that will give you the blend appropriate to your planting program. If your containers receive frequent spring and fall rains, use perlite rather than vermiculite. If your mix is to be used for shrubs and trees, use a combination of $1/3$ sand and $2/3$ ground bark or peat moss.

The mixing process is the same for all mixes. To make a cubic yard of mix, take one of the recipes recommended on pages 25 and 26, or, for example, this even more basic one:

> 14 cubic feet of peat moss, nitrogen-stabilized fir bark or pine bark, and
> 14 cubic feet of vermiculite or perlite.

Dump the ingredients in a pile and roughly mix them. Dampen the mix as you go. (Dry peat moss is far easier to wet with warm water than with tap water.)

Spread these fertilizer elements over the rough mix:

> 5 pounds of ground limestone
> 5 pounds of 5-10-10 fertilizer

Note: *Read the label. In addition to nitrogen, fertilizer should contain phosphorus and potash (potassium), limestone, calcium, magnesium, sulphur, iron, manganese, and zinc.*

Use a scoop shovel to mix the ingredients into a cone-shaped pile, letting each shovelful dribble down the cone. To mix thoroughly, it's best to rebuild the cone three to five times (see illustration).

If you don't intend to use the mix soon after making it, store it in plastic bags or plastic garbage cans. To mix smaller quantities, reduce the amounts of the ingredients proportionately.

Note: *One cubic yard equals 27 cubic feet or 22 bushels. However, 15 to 20 percent shrinkage occurs in mixing because of loss of air space. For 1 full yard of mix, use an additional 4 bushels, or 5 cubic feet. To obtain 1 full yard of mix, use 26 bushels or 32 cubic feet.*

5. The final mix is ready to use or can be stored if it is completely dry.

If you are concerned about salt build-up, or if you suspect you have overfertilized, leach out the excess. This can be done by running a hose in the pot on low pressure for 10–15 minutes.

Fertilizer—When and How Much To Use

If you plan to use a mix containing a 5-10-10 fertilizer, normally you should begin applying it three weeks after planting. If you need to water frequently after planting, start the feeding program earlier.

Because watering leaches fertilizers through the mixes, how often you water determines how often you should fertilize. Moreover, since fertilizers will leach from mixtures containing perlite faster than from those containing vermiculite, plants grown in a peat moss/perlite mix will require more frequent applications of fertilizer.

Some container gardeners prefer to fertilize with a weak nutrient solution, applying it with every other irrigation. If you choose this method, use only ⅕ the amount of fertilizer called for on the label for a monthly application. That is, if the label calls for 1 tablespoon to a gallon of water, use 1 tablespoon, as specified, but increase the dilution by using 5 gallons of water.

You need to pay closer attention to plants growing in containers than to the same plants growing in a flower border or in a vegetable patch. Because of the limited volume in a container the soil tends to dry out faster than in the garden, so you must compensate for the smaller root area by watering and feeding more frequently.

No plant requires a large amount of fertilizer at any one time, but it does need to be fed continually. The nutrient solution applications just described satisfy the plant's need for a constant supply of nutrients. Time-release fertilizers are another popular method of meeting this need. As the plant receives water, these fertilizers are released in small amounts. (Check the labels for rate of application.) The easiest method is to use a time-release fertilizer mixed with the soil.

Garden Soils and Container Soils

The organic materials used in the commercial synthetic mixes decompose slowly. In any commercial container mix, peat moss, redwood sawdust, fir bark, and pine bark are surprisingly stable. Some of our container plants grow in a mix of fir bark and sand that has held up for five years.

Converting garden soil into container soil. To condition a garden soil, you can add all types of organic material—peat moss, ground bark, manure, leaf mold, and compost, in all stages of decay. All organic materials help make heavy soils more friable and sandy soils more able to retain water and nutrients. Manure and compost perform the additional service of increasing the fertility of the soil. If you're using organic amendments such as these, or organic mulches of leaves, straw, or grass clippings, it's a good idea to add organic matter to the soil every year to replace that which has broken down.

Be careful not to use materials that shrink or disappear in your container mix. A garden soil of clay loam or sandy loam, mixed with either peat moss, nitrogen-stabilized sawdust, or ground bark, will give you the most satisfactory mix.

Since the purpose of adding organic matter is to change the physical structure of the soil, adding a little dab of this or that won't do the job—a little peat moss or a little straw and compressed clay soil makes only a good adobe brick. Instead, top a garden soil with a 2-inch layer of ground bark, rototill it into the top 2 inches of soil, and you'll have a really useful container soil. Water will drain through it rapidly; it will have the right amount of air space after irrigation; and it will retain water sufficiently for good plant growth.

Use of Waste Products

Synthetic mixes may use organic ingredients that once were classed as waste products—fir bark, pine bark, and redwood sawdust. Although these particular ingredients have been thoroughly tested for toxicity, pH reaction, and uniformity, other waste products also can be used. The fewer green materials

Leaf mold. Leaves that are composted in the fall should, if properly handled, be partially decomposed and ready for use by spring. This is a particularly good mulch or additive for acid-loving plants such as azaleas, rhododendrons, and some ferns.

Straw. Used primarily for winter protection, straw can also be used as a summer mulch to cool soils. It's highly flammable and should not be used where a cigarette could be carelessly dropped.

Sawdust. This is a very common mulch, but a nitrogen deficiency almost always occurs in the soil after unfortified sawdust is applied. It is important that you apply a nitrogen fertilizer regularly. Reports of toxic materials in sawdust have not been substantiated by research.

Strawy manure. Manure makes an excellent mulch or soil amendment if it has been partially decomposed. Fresh manure can burn tender roots. Also, be sure that it has not been treated with odor-reducing chemicals, which can be injurious to growing plants. No nitrogen need be added to manure.

Pomace (apple or grape). Pomace is the spent seeds and skins of apples or grapes—a by-product of cider and wine making. Studies of grape pomace have shown that it is a slow-to-decompose soil amendment that adds small amounts of nitrogen to the soil over a sustained period.

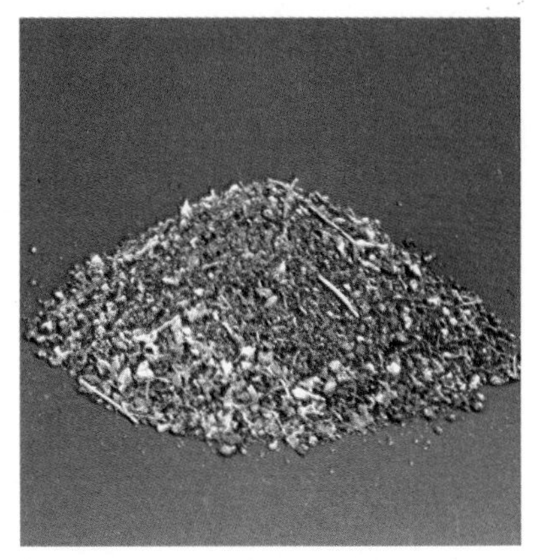

Compost. You can make an excellent soil amendment at home by composting various kinds of non-woody refuse such as grass clippings, leaves, and plant tops from vegetables or the flower garden. When partially decomposed, this material makes one of the best organic mulches.

you burn or bury, the more waste products you will have for use. You might explore your area for specialized waste products—grape pomace where grapes are pressed; nut shells where nuts are shelled.

"What comes out of the soil should go back into the soil," say conservationists. But gardeners don't always agree. While it's true that crushed almond shells, as well as grape pomace (when composted) can be used safely as a soil amendment, walnut leaves or crushed walnut shells will poison the soil for garden plants. Sunflower seed hulls look promising, but tests have proven that they contain some growth-inhibiting properties. Any organic material, especially agricultural by-products, must be tested carefully to ensure that it contains no toxic elements.

For More Information

If you wish to dig deep into the subject of soil mixes for growing plants in containers, this publication will be of help.

Cornell Peat-Lite Mixes for Commercial Plant Growing. Information Bulletin 43, by James W. Boodley and Raymond Sheldrake, Jr. Send 25¢ to: Cooperative Extension, New York State College of Agriculture, Cornell University, Ithaca, NY 14853.

Planting and Transplanting

When using lightweight synthetic mixes, it's best to wet the mix before using it. The easiest and least messy way is to add water directly to the plastic bag the mix comes in. Hold the top of the bag and knead the water in until the mixture is evenly moist. Letting the entire bag sit overnight before using will further ensure an even distribution of moisture throughout the mixture. (A pot filled with dry mix is difficult to wet properly.) Then fill the container, firming the mix down, especially near the edges. Make sure to water the plants thoroughly after transplanting. If you don't plan to use all the mix immediately, keep it moist by tying the top of the bag tightly.

Push up with
thumb or finger.

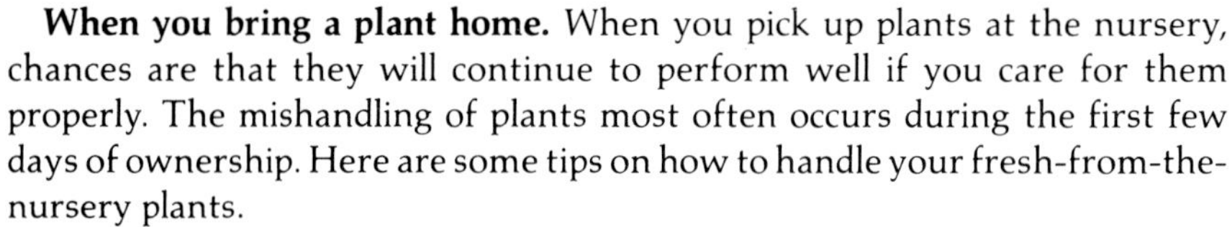

When you bring a plant home. When you pick up plants at the nursery, chances are that they will continue to perform well if you care for them properly. The mishandling of plants most often occurs during the first few days of ownership. Here are some tips on how to handle your fresh-from-the-nursery plants.

If you run out of time to plant all your choices and must hold some plants over for the following weekend, make sure that they don't dry out in the interim. Water them as you would any container plant until you are ready to remove them from the nursery containers. A damp (not wet) rootball will not shatter or stick to the edge of the container.

Remove the plants from cell packs and market packs (2 to 12 plants in a flat) the easy way: squeeze the bottom of the container in the cell pack to force the rootball above the lip. When removing plants from market trays, cut the soil in blocks. Use a putty knife for cutting soil and removing the rootball.

Don't pull plants out of containers. Plants are grown in plastic, fiber, and metal containers. Ask the nursery to cut straight-sided cans. However, plants grown in cans, pots, or tubs with sloping sides can be tapped out of the container. Hold the container upside down, and tap it against a ledge. Hold the rootball with the plant stem between your fingers.

Cut off wrapping that shows above the surface.

Handle the so-called biodegradable containers carefully. Small-sized plants may come in peat pots, Jiffy 7's, or paper pots; larger-sized shrubs may come in fiber pots, or balled and burlapped (B & B). Plant peat pots and Jiffy 7's below the soil line. With peat pots, punch holes in the bottom and remove the upper exposed edges of the container. The rootball dries out quickly if any part of the peat pot or wrapping remains above the soil surface.

Root prune when necessary. If roots have formed outside the rootball along the sides and bottom of the container, remove them before setting the plant into the larger container. The pruning will speed up the formation of new roots and the penetration of roots into the soil surrounding the rootball. If the plant is pot-bound and the roots have formed a solid mass that you cannot loosen by hand, make four or five cuts from top to bottom with a sharp knife down the side of the rootball and then run your finger through the cuts to fray the roots.

Set a root-pruned plant into the container soil at the level it grew in the nursery. Firm the soil around the rootball and water thoroughly. Keep the rootball moist until the roots have spread into the surrounding soil. Soil differences may make the rootball dry out even though the surrounding soil is wet.

Pot-bound plant

Too high Too low Just right

Screen over hole

Watering. After placing the plant in a container, thoroughly water the soil mass. The soil, after settling, should be ½ to 1 inch below the rim of the can to allow *one* application of water to moisten the rootball and drain through the container. If the watering space is too shallow, you may have to water, let it drain into the soil, and then water again.

It's advisable to use a mulch of bark chunks, pea gravel, or marble chips, or a ground cover such as alyssum, ajuga, or vinca over the soil in a large container. Not only will this dress up the planting and slow down evaporation, but it also will keep the planting soil from being disturbed when you water.

How frequently you should water depends upon: the soil mix; the type and size of container; temperatures; wind; sunlight; and humidity.

Some plants advertise their need for water by wilting quite drastically. But once watered, many of them—impatiens, strawberries, and tomatoes, for instance—make an equally dramatic and speedy recovery.

Don't water by the calendar. A plant that needs water every day during a stretch of warm sunny days can go on an every-other-day schedule in cloudy weather.

This severely wilted piggyback plant *(Tolmiea menziesii)* showed its dramatic powers of recovery when water was applied. Within three hours it was photographed as shown on the right.

One of the great values of the synthetic soil mixes is that they can't become waterlogged if the container drains properly.

A plant in a porous clay pot will need water more frequently than one in a plastic or glazed pot. Some gardeners solve the evaporation problem by placing the pot within a larger pot and insulating the space between the two with peat moss or perlite and layers of charcoal and/or gravel. If you do this, be careful not to overwater, or the insulation will become soaked.

With small pots, one way to solve the evaporation problem is to group them together in a wooden box. A 14″ × 24″ box that's 10 inches deep will hold two 5-gallon-sized containers, or a group of 6-inch pots. Put ground bark or peat moss between the pots (this also acts as a mulch).

Drip-irrigation hardware permits many types of container-watering systems. Here, a length of plastic pipe with a half-dozen spaghetti tubes with drip spitters attached delivers the constant but minute amount of water the containers need. It's one way to "vacationize" your garden.

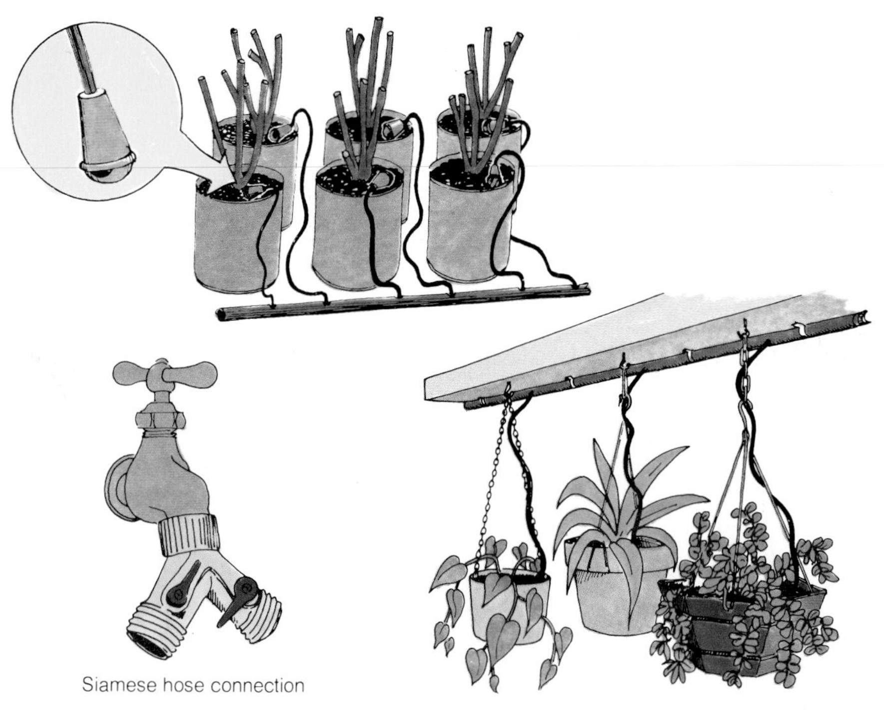

Siamese hose connection

Watering devices can make life easier for the container gardener. The Siamese hose connector with double shut-offs lets you set up a permanent watering system for containers without having to fiddle with hose bibbs.

Mist spray nozzles give many container plants the fog they need on dry hot days.

Mist spray nozzles

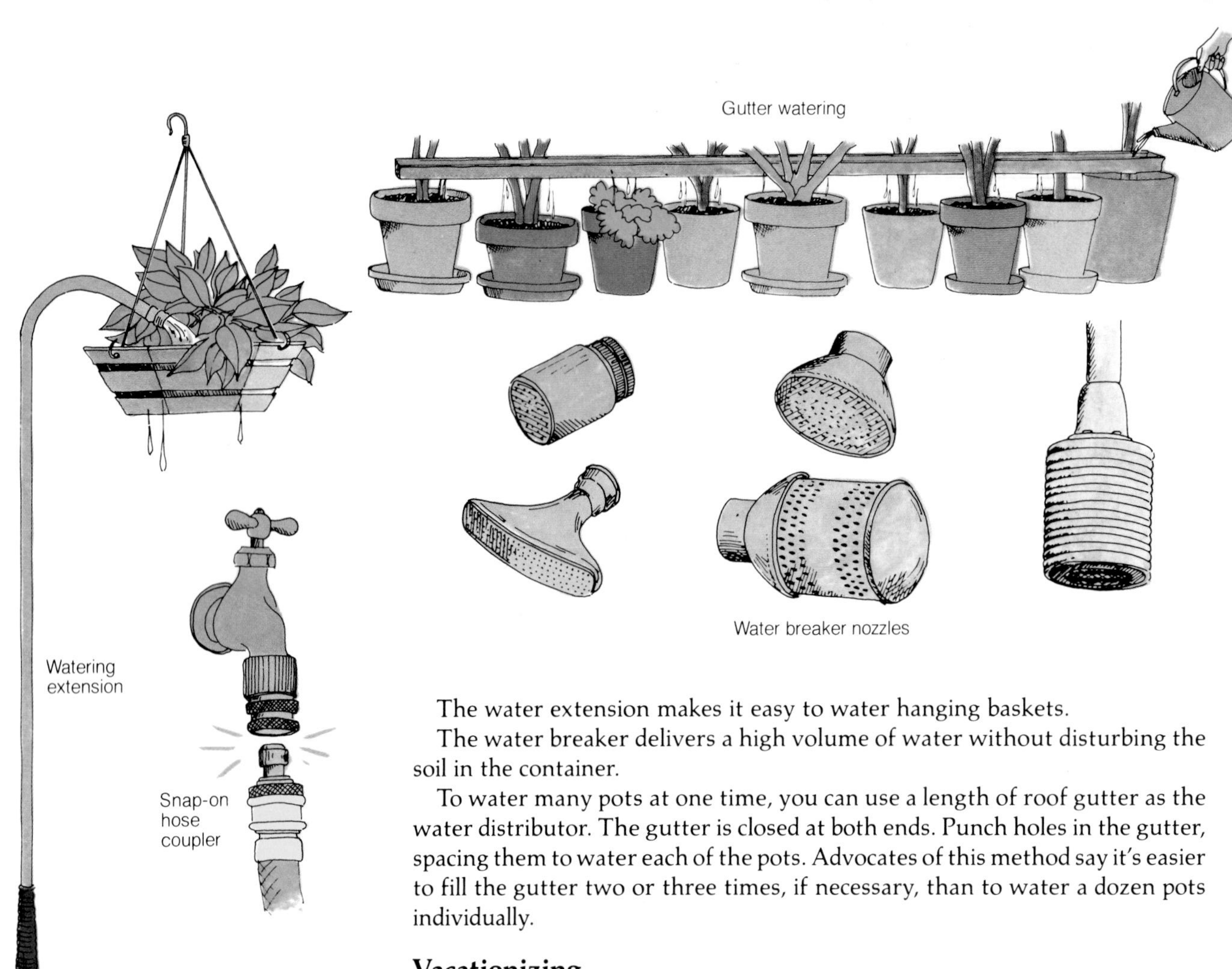

The water extension makes it easy to water hanging baskets.

The water breaker delivers a high volume of water without disturbing the soil in the container.

To water many pots at one time, you can use a length of roof gutter as the water distributor. The gutter is closed at both ends. Punch holes in the gutter, spacing them to water each of the pots. Advocates of this method say it's easier to fill the gutter two or three times, if necessary, than to water a dozen pots individually.

Vacationizing

Can your plants get along without you for a long weekend? For a week? Regardless of which watering system you use—automatic, drip, or wick—a plant sitter or at least an occasional visit from a friendly neighbor is a necessity if you plan to be away for a week or more. Even the most sophisticated watering systems need attention. However, you can make the plant sitter's watering job less burdensome in several ways.

Move the containers into a single watering spot, one where they will be protected from the wind and direct sun. Sun-loving plants can take filtered shade for a week or two. Grouping plants together forms a mutual protection society, one plant protecting another.

Wick watering will take care of watering needs for a week or more. Put one end of the wick in a pail of water and the other in the soil of the container. This will give the container a continuous supply of water. You can use wicks of glass wool, fraying the ends that go into the soil, or a nylon clothesline. Special wicks also are available.

You can build a two-compartment planter box that can be watered and fed with wicks. The upper compartment holds the soil and plants; the lower compartment has a metal gutter that holds water with a nutrient solution for wick watering and feeding the plants.

To create a water reservoir for a number of wick-watered pots, you can use large, custom-made pans of sheet metal, or homemade wooden boxes made watertight and filled with gravel.

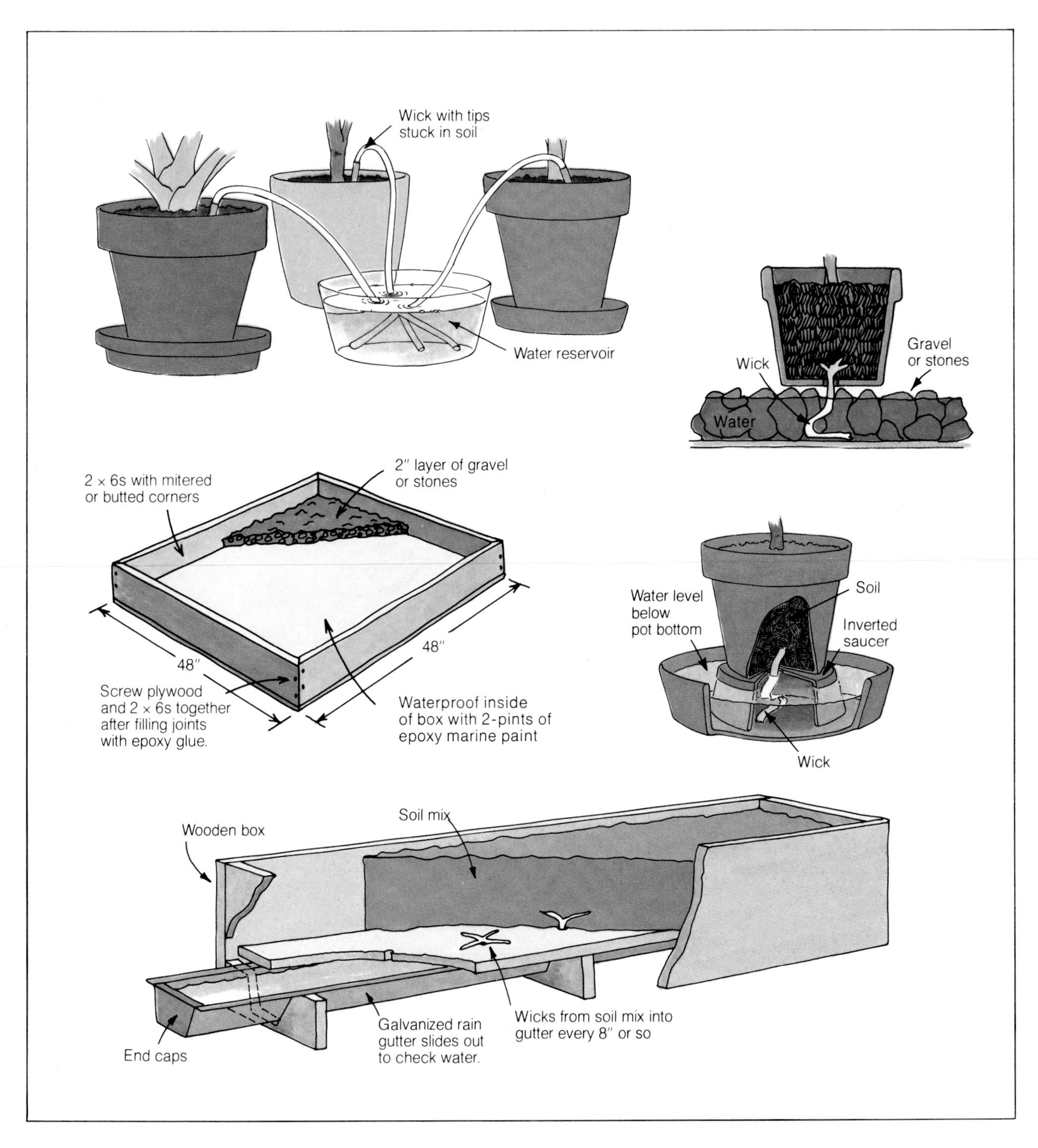

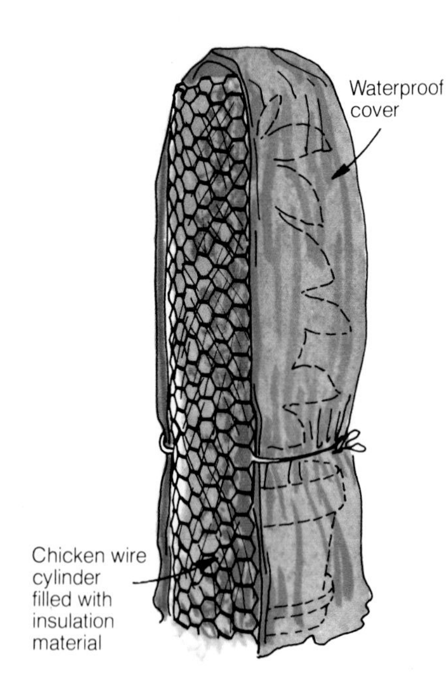

Winterizing

You can protect even the most vulnerable plants from the cold by wrapping the plant and the container in a chicken-wire cylinder, filling the cylinder with insulating material (e.g., hay, straw, or dried leaves), and keeping it dry with a waterproof cover.

Don't remove this covering too soon in spring—much frost damage occurs when balmy days are followed by cold windy nights.

Weight

The use of a lightweight soil mix—peat moss and perlite or vermiculite—lessens the weight problem. But a moist mix weighs far more than a dry one.

For moving large, heavy tubs, a dolly on casters is a welcome aid. In fact, it pays to attach a set of casters to the base of any large box or tub. Not only do casters make the container easier to move, but they also create air space beneath the container, robbing earwigs and slugs of a potential hiding place.

If you have a great many containers, you'll find a handtruck to be a useful gadget. Attaching a trash bag to the handtruck lightens the chore of garden clean-up.

Roll Rather Than Lift.

To move planters and boxes that are too heavy to lift easily, use rollers of pipe or wood. A set of three or four wood dowels, 2 or 3 inches in diameter, will do the trick.

Wooden Containers

If the bottom of a wooden container is in direct contact with a moist surface, eventually it will rot. All planters, tubs, and boxes should have air space beneath them. If the box or tub you buy or build doesn't have "feet," use small wooden blocks to keep the container an inch or so aboveground.

You can treat wooden containers inside and at the bottom with a wood preservative containing copper sulfate, such as "Cuprinol" or "Copper Green." Flow it on with brush or spray. Do not use wood preservatives containing pentachlorophenol, such as "Wood Life" or "Penta-treat"—they are toxic to plants. Remember to seal the edges when treating exterior plywood.

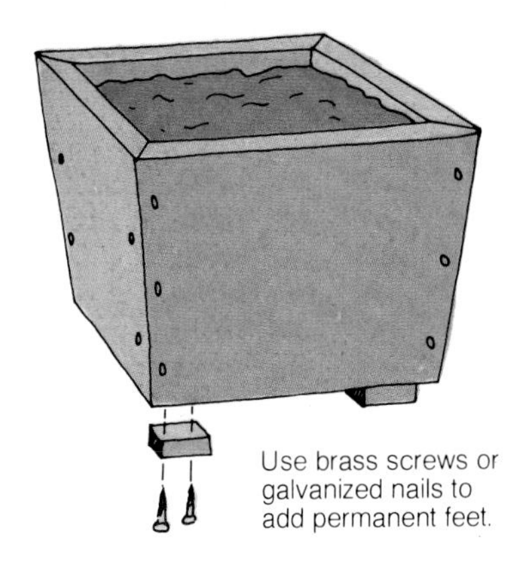
Use brass screws or galvanized nails to add permanent feet.

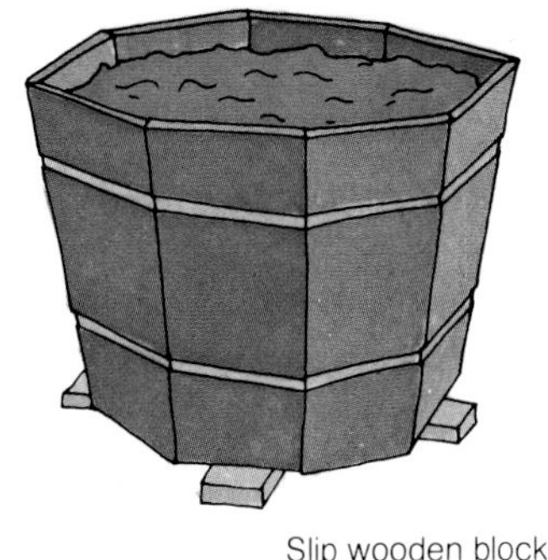
Slip wooden blocks underneath for temporary "feet."

Eliminating Insects in Containers

Just because plants are in containers doesn't mean they are immune from insect damage. Says one experienced container gardener:

"Container gardens have many advantages, but they also may invite such pests as slugs, snails, earwigs, and sow bugs. The moist atmosphere of the containers offers a haven, like an oasis on the desert, to these moisture-seeking pests. Instead of sprinkling bait on the soil, literally sending out an invitation to any slugs or snails to climb into the pot and have a feast, place some pellets on a fresh, damp lettuce leaf and set it near the pot. Do this in the early evening after wetting the areas surrounding and underneath the containers. The following morning it is easy to pick up your 'catch' and dump it into the trash. Repeat the procedure for three consecutive evenings, then again about every ten days until the problem is eliminated.

"Earwig bait should be handled in the same manner. Additional baiting can be effective for earwigs by providing some rolled-up newspaper that holds some bait for any daytime munchers. They normally hide during the daylight hours, and the darkness of the rolled-up newspapers is an attraction for them."

Since container plants must be watered frequently, you'll be inspecting them frequently, which means that you'll have a good chance of noticing—and dealing with—the initial insect attack.

Snail bait on a damp lettuce leaf

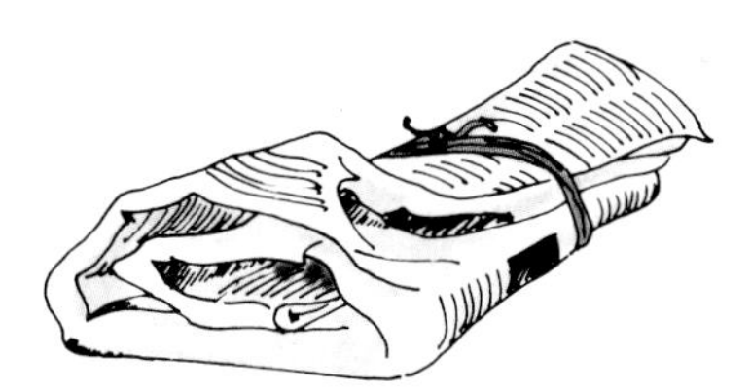
Earwig bait in a rolled newspaper

Begonia, fuchsia, and nasturtium hanging above bright red impatiens.

HANGING BASKETS

There is a wide variety of materials and plants suitable for hanging baskets, so you can match the shapes, sizes, colors, and textures of the containers and the plants to their location.

Hanging plants bring an added dimension to many landscaping and interior situations. On decks and patios or inside such garden structures as arbors, gazebos, and pergolas, hanging plants can highlight (or disguise) some interesting (or unattractive) detail. They can also help to define the space visually. If they are lightweight, and they should be, hanging baskets can be moved from place to place indoors or outdoors, for special occasions.

Where space is limited, hanging baskets may be a necessity. You can accommodate many more plants by getting some off the floor and also avoid the monotony of having everything on one level.

Before you decide what plants you want to hang (see pages 40-45), consider the container itself. Remember, too, that they should be kept light enough to lift even when they are soaking wet.

A container's appearance always matters, but when the container is used as a hanging basket, its function becomes equally important. When hanging, a container needs more protection from sun and wind than it would on the ground. When the common clay pot is exposed on all sides to the movement of air, it becomes an efficient evaporative unit, and either requires a waterproof cover or else much more frequent watering.

Wood, fortunately, is relatively impervious to water. However, its ability to be shaped is limited.

Wire, a conveniently malleable material, can be lined with sphagnum moss in baskets and columnar shapes to create a living bouquet. Moss has an appealing, natural, green-garden look, but it too must be watered regularly. Many other materials can be used instead of sphagnum moss, or in addition to it, and the following pages illustrate various ways in which to assemble your living "bouquet."

However you choose to put together your hanging basket, it is very important that you leave enough watering space at the top. Fill the basket with soil only up to ½ inch below the top, not up to the very top. Pack the sphagnum moss in thick and tight around the top inch of the basket. This creates a watering basin that allows the soil in the container to get thoroughly wet when you water (which should be daily—sometimes even twice a day). And use one heavy application of water to wet the soil, or else you'll have to keep watering in small amounts three or four times a day in order to get a good soaking.

Keeping the basket neat and in full color requires continual grooming. Remove all spent blooms. Prune off straying shoots. Use a few old-fashioned hairpins to pin shoots or vines to the moss. A colorful hanging basket demands attention from the basket-tender as well as from the viewer.

When frost or age have put an end to a basket's good looks, take it to the compost pile or the work section of the garden and turn it upside down. Peel the layer of sphagnum moss off the root ball and save the moss and the wire for later reuse. Just clean the moss of any foreign material, soil, or plant roots, and use it to build a new basket with fresh soil.

Here's how one gardener puts together a hanging basket. The top rim is tightly packed with moss (Step 2 below).

Garden shears are used to trim off straggly moss for a neater look (Step 5 below).

The rootball is carefully inserted through the hole in the moss (Step 7 below).

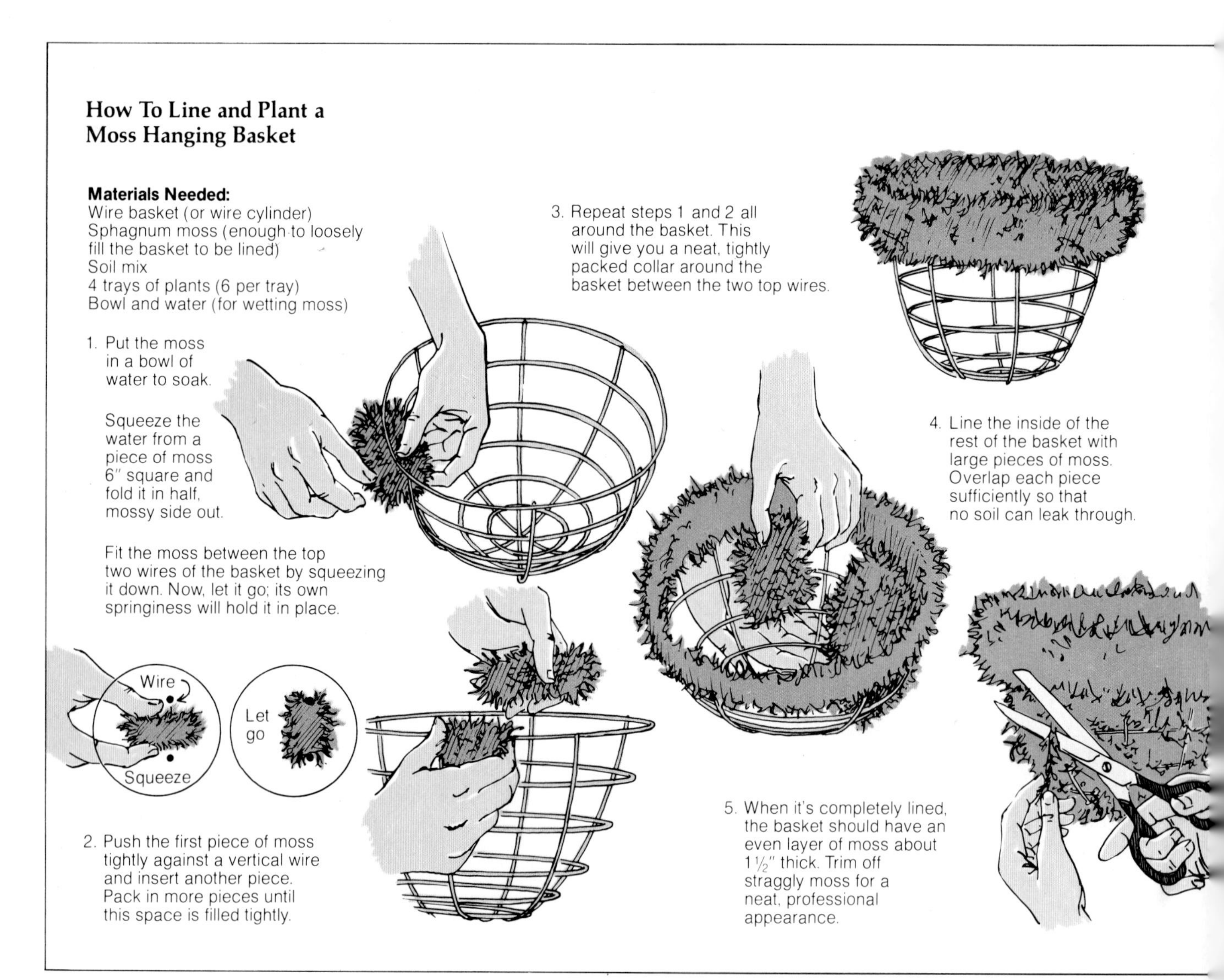

How To Line and Plant a Moss Hanging Basket

Materials Needed:
Wire basket (or wire cylinder)
Sphagnum moss (enough to loosely fill the basket to be lined)
Soil mix
4 trays of plants (6 per tray)
Bowl and water (for wetting moss)

1. Put the moss in a bowl of water to soak.

   Squeeze the water from a piece of moss 6" square and fold it in half, mossy side out.

   Fit the moss between the top two wires of the basket by squeezing it down. Now, let it go; its own springiness will hold it in place.

2. Push the first piece of moss tightly against a vertical wire and insert another piece. Pack in more pieces until this space is filled tightly.

3. Repeat steps 1 and 2 all around the basket. This will give you a neat, tightly packed collar around the basket between the two top wires.

4. Line the inside of the rest of the basket with large pieces of moss. Overlap each piece sufficiently so that no soil can leak through.

5. When it's completely lined, the basket should have an even layer of moss about 1 ½" thick. Trim off straggly moss for a neat, professional appearance.

Wire baskets, usually filled with sphagnum moss, come in many shapes and sizes. The half-round ones are for attaching to flat surfaces.

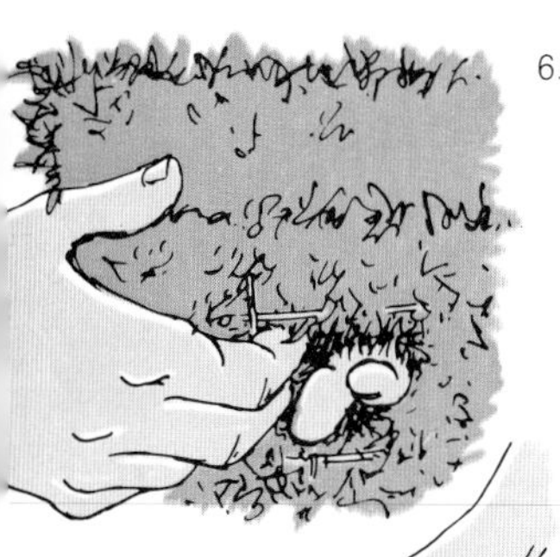

6. Place the moist soil mix in the first 1½" of the bottom. Poke your fingers through from both sides at soil level and work a hole large enough to insert a plant. Spread the wire, if necessary.

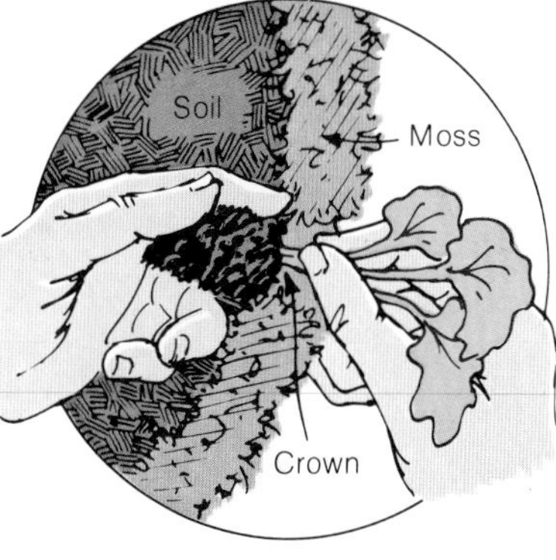

7. Insert each plant so its root ball lies on the soil mix surface and the crown of the plant is even with the inside of the moss lining.

8. When the first row of plants is in place, cover it with 1" or 2" of soil mix, then add another row of plants. Keep layering soil and plants until you reach the collar of moss at the top.

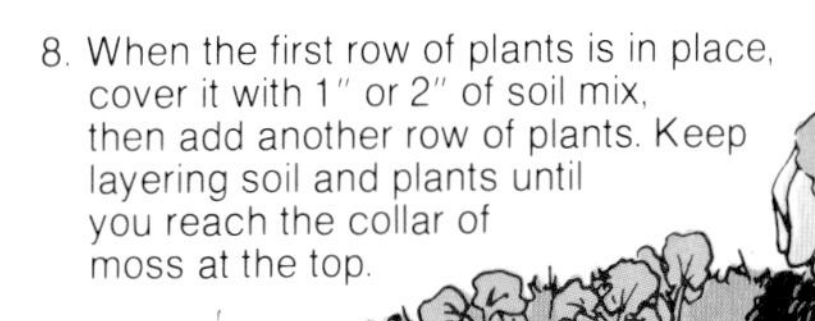

9. Finally, fill all but about an inch of the basket with soil mix and plant the top as you would a flower pot. Insert several plants, using about the same spacing as on the sides.

Alternative Ways of Planting

Here are two other methods of planting in a moss basket. Choose whichever is best for you.

1. Poke holes and push all the plants through the moss where you want them. Then fill the basket with soil mix all at once and plant the top (as described earlier).

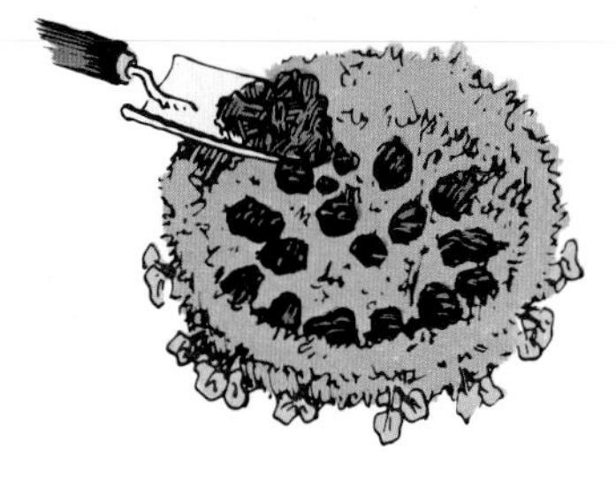

2. Or fill the entire basket with soil mix. Then poke holes through the moss into the soil and insert the plants.

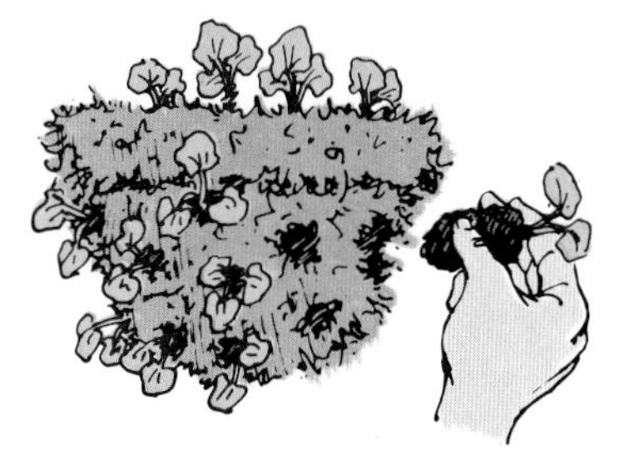

Planting a Plastic "Hanging Basket"

Materials Needed:

10" plastic pot
Soil mix
7 or 8 plants
Plastic film or sphagnum moss

1. Make four or five 1½"-diameter holes in the sides of the pot, either by drilling and enlarging with a hand rasp, or by burning with a hot metal pipe or soldering iron. Be sure there are drain holes in the bottom.

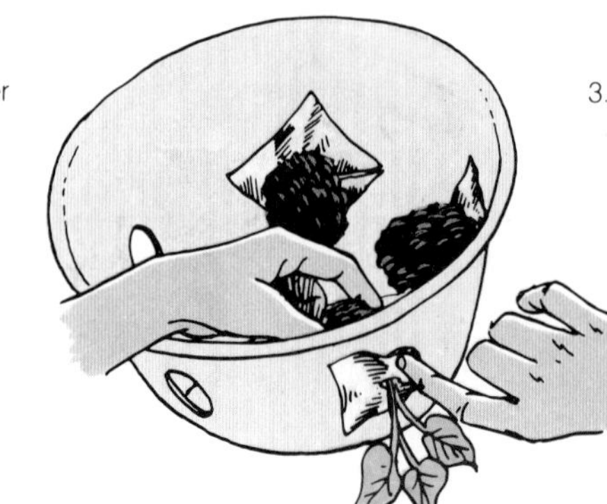

3. Tuck the plastic into the holes as you put the plants through. This will keep the soil from spilling out. Sphagnum moss wrapped around the stem works well, too.

Plastic film

2. Cut a 3" square of plastic film, as shown.

Slip the plastic around the stems of your plants.

4. Fill the basket with soil mix and add the remaining plants to the top. Water thoroughly.

A Three-Piece "Hanging Basket"

This hanging basket has a unique construction that makes it a "snap" to plant.

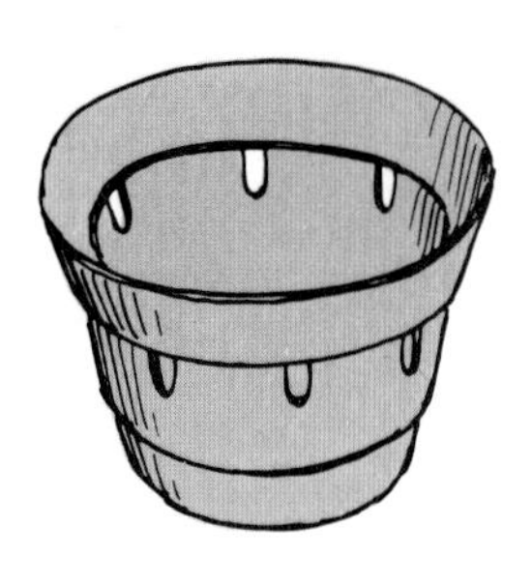

The upper ring

The bottom pot

The saucer

1. Fill with soil mix up to the slots. Lay the plants on the soil and put the stems through the slots.

2. Snap on the top ring. Add soil mix to within an inch or so of the rim and plant the remaining plants in the top.

3. Snap on the saucer and water thoroughly.

The barber-pole basket on the left, with stripes of Irish moss and Spanish moss ground covers, and the fibrous begonia display above, show two distinct ways of using a wire cylinder.

Here are the steps to a hanging arrangement in a cylinder. The green indoor/outdoor carpet, used as a liner, mostly disappears. If water-holding liners are used, extra drainage holes should be drilled in the wood base.

This cylinder is lined with a carpet mulch inlaid with bark chunks.

Planting in Driftwood

Handsomely twisted driftwood or tree branches can make beautiful planting containers.

Decide where you want your planting pocket. A concave curve or the space between two or more branches is the easiest (and probably the most attractive, too).

Note: If your driftwood comes from the ocean, before planting soak it in fresh water for several days to remove the salt.

Materials Needed:
Piece of driftwood
Chicken wire
Galvanized fence
staples (staple-gun
staples rust)
Sphagnum moss
Soil mix

1. Cut and form the wire to the shape you want and staple it securely to the wood. Leave an opening at the top for inserting the moss and soil.
2. Line the wire with sphagnum moss. Overlap the pieces so the soil cannot leak out.
3. Fill the pocket with soil mix and plant.
4. Add a heavy-duty screw eye and hang it up.

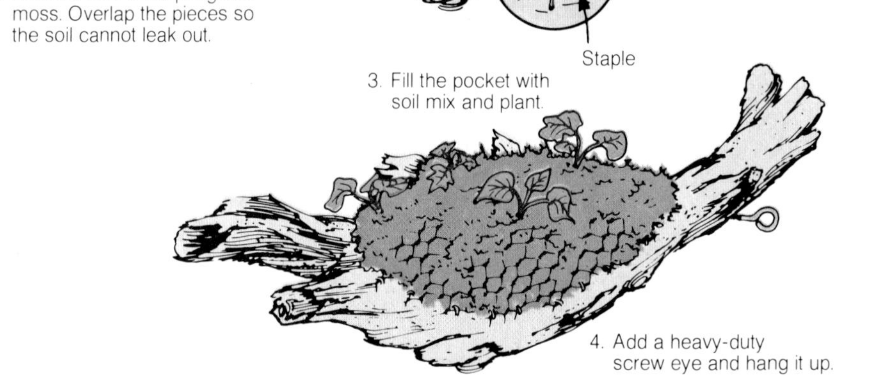

Planting in a Log Round

1. Rout (hollow out) the center to a depth of about 1" and drill some drain holes.

2. Add soil mix and plant.

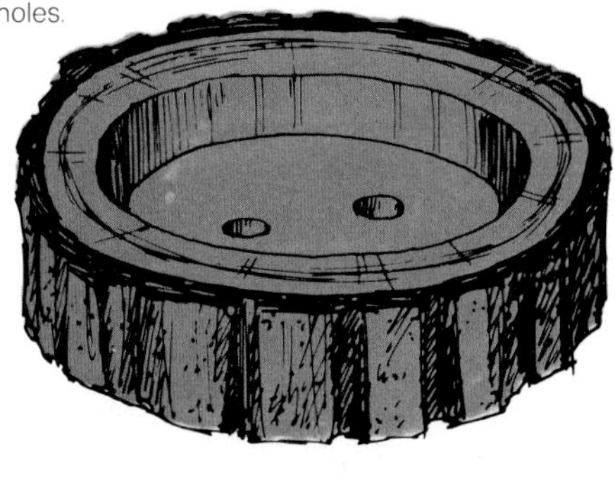

3. Or don't hollow out the center. Use chicken wire and sphagnum moss to plant on top (similar to the driftwood planter).

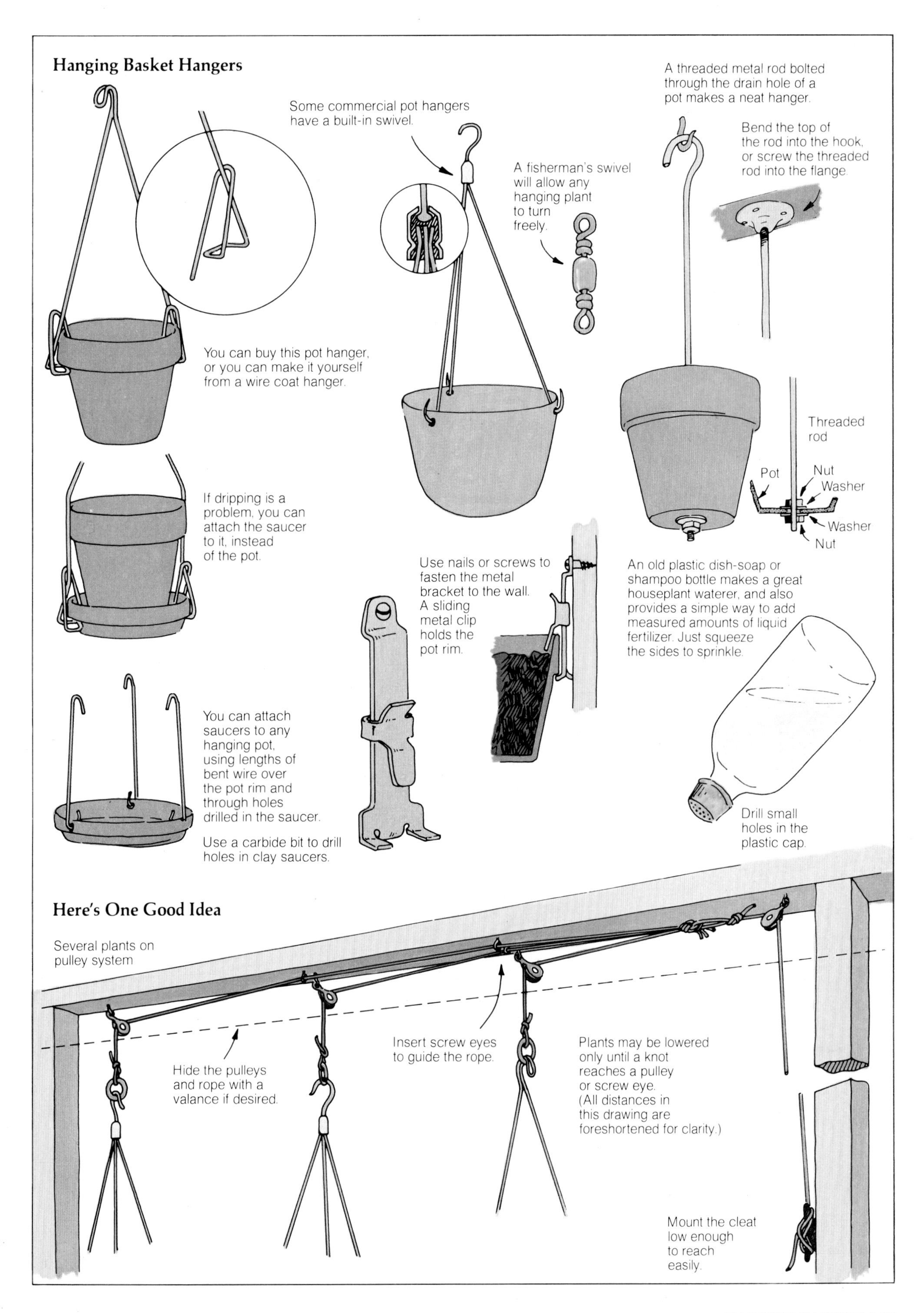
Hanging Basket Hangers
Some commercial pot hangers have a built-in swivel.
A threaded metal rod bolted through the drain hole of a pot makes a neat hanger.
Bend the top of the rod into the hook, or screw the threaded rod into the flange.
A fisherman's swivel will allow any hanging plant to turn freely.
You can buy this pot hanger, or you can make it yourself from a wire coat hanger.
Threaded rod
Pot
Nut
Washer
Washer
Nut
If dripping is a problem, you can attach the saucer to it, instead of the pot.
Use nails or screws to fasten the metal bracket to the wall. A sliding metal clip holds the pot rim.
An old plastic dish-soap or shampoo bottle makes a great houseplant waterer, and also provides a simple way to add measured amounts of liquid fertilizer. Just squeeze the sides to sprinkle.
You can attach saucers to any hanging pot, using lengths of bent wire over the pot rim and through holes drilled in the saucer.
Use a carbide bit to drill holes in clay saucers.
Drill small holes in the plastic cap.
Here's One Good Idea
Several plants on pulley system
Hide the pulleys and rope with a valance if desired.
Insert screw eyes to guide the rope.
Plants may be lowered only until a knot reaches a pulley or screw eye. (All distances in this drawing are foreshortened for clarity.)
Mount the cleat low enough to reach easily.

Plants for Hanging Baskets

The following bulbs, vines, ground covers, and shrubs have a habit of drooping growth and are excellent for hanging baskets. The chart on pages 52-59 includes some annual plants that will do well briefly in hanging baskets.

Achimenes. This tender bulb produces flowers for spring and summer color and is ideal for hanging baskets or other containers in partially shaded locations. The 'Cascade' varieties are exceptional for hanging-basket displays. Flower colors include blue, pink, rose, purple, light yellow, orange, crimson, and red. Plant three to five bulbs per 12-inch basket. The bulbs will require a few months of rest after the foliage dies; store in a cool, dry location for the winter months.

Asparagus fern. This is not a true fern, but its display of foliage is just as attractive as that of its namesake. The best asparagus fern for hanging baskets is the "Sprengeri" asparagus, with arching stems that provide cascades of lush green color. Its needle-like foliage has a heavy texture and is borne in clusters along the stems. A vigorous grower, the plant requires periodic pruning of old stems to provide room for new shoots. Grow it in full sun or partial shade where summers are hot. Bring it indoors in cold-winter areas. The plant is hardy to 20°F.

Aubrieta *(Aubrieta deltoidea).* A low-growing perennial with silver-green foliage and spring flowers of red, pink, or lavender, aubrieta requires light shearing after flowering (never cut back more than half the growth). A sunny exposure is best; in hot areas, however, it requires partial shade. The plant is good with Basket-of-Gold, and is hardy in all areas.

Basket-of-Gold *(Aurinia saxatilis,* formerly called *Alyssum saxatile).* A hardy perennial that will provide color in spring and early summer. Hang it in full sun for a mass display of golden-yellow color. Good with other sun-loving plants. Lightly trim the plants after they've bloomed, removing no more than half the growth. Basket-of-Gold is hardy in all areas.

Achimenes

Asparagus fern (*A.* 'Myers')

Basket-of-Gold (*Aurinia saxatilis*)

Tuberous begonias hang to the left and right of a fuchsia.

Begonia, tuberous (*B.* × *tuberhybrida* Pendula group). This special group, designated as "Hanging Basket Begonias," offers a wide variety of glamorous flower forms and colors. Colors include white, yellow, pink, orange, red, and various bicolor patterns. Begonias flower from summer to fall in partial or full shade. The tubers must be dug up at the end of the flowering season and stored in a cool, dry location until the next season's planting.

Bougainvillea. This showy plant performs best in warm-winter climates but can be adapted to colder areas if given winter protection. In areas of frequent frost, protect it by placing it against a warm wall, or move it indoors. Where summer temperatures are high, grow in partial shade; otherwise grow in full sun. Pinch frequently to encourage bushiness. With its dark green leaves and masses of glowing red flowers, 'Crimson Jewel' makes a good hanging-basket specimen.

Candytuft

Camellia *(C. hiemalis).* Two varieties, formerly in the *C. sasanqua* class, make attractive hanging-basket plantings: 'Showa No Sakae' (pink semi-double flowers) and 'Shishi Gashira' (rose-red double flowers). Both have graceful, arched branch patterns and are continuously in bloom from October to March. Flower production is reduced by a combination of cold weather and abundant rain, conditions that exist in parts of California and the Northwest. For best results in such situations, grow these camellias under an overhang or similar protection.

Candytuft *(Iberis sempervirens).* Not to be confused with its annual cousin, *I. umbellata*, this evergreen perennial makes an attractive basket: its foliage serves as a contrasting background for its snow-white flowers. Flowering occurs in early spring and literally covers the plant. After it has flowered, it requires only a light trimming to stimulate compact growth. It prefers full sun, although partial shade also is suitable. Candytuft is hardy in all areas.

Cotoneaster. Within the genus *Cotoneaster*, two species adapt well to growing in baskets: creeping cotoneaster (*C. adpressus*) and bearberry cotoneaster (*C. dammeri*). Creeping cotoneaster is a slow-growing, deciduous shrub that grows to a height of 12 inches and bears pink flowers followed by bright red berries. The bearberry cotoneaster also provides a cascading display of white flowers and red berries. It has evergreen foliage and reaches a height of 6 inches. Grow cotoneaster in full sun or partial shade. It is hardy in all areas.

Euonymus. Many varieties of *E. fortunei* make hardy ground covers, and their wide-spreading habit works for hanging baskets, as well. Keep wayward branches pruned when grown in hanging baskets. The purple-leafed wintercreeper variety, 'Colorata', will drape nicely, as will the green and white variegated form, 'Gracilis'. Grow in full sun or partial shade. Euonymus is hardy in all areas.

Indoors or outdoors, ferns are naturals in hanging baskets. And they like the shade.

Fern. The fern's familiar lush green form, with its arching, drooping fronds, makes it very effective in hanging containers. Of the many kinds to choose from, the *Davallia* species are favorites, also known as Rabbit's foot or Squirrel's foot ferns because of their fuzzy, creeping rhizomes. Intricately cut, airy fronds grow from the rhizomes, and make them appear to be more delicate than they really are. They are especially beautiful in hanging baskets. *Nephrolepis exaltata* 'Bostoniensis', the popular Boston fern, will develop spreading fronds that drape as long as 5 feet when grown in favorable conditions. 'Fluffy Ruffles', 'Verona', 'Whitmanii', and 'Smithii' are other cultivars of this old standby. They differ from one another in the texture and division of the fronds. During the warm months, grow them outdoors in filtered shade protected from direct sun, harsh winds, and unexpected frosts. Water frequently. Bring them indoors in winter and place them in a north or east window, away from direct sun. Plants respond well to frequent misting.

Above: The Italian Bellflower blooms prolifically.
Right: Fuchsias prefer cool-summer climates and should be protected from hot winds.

Fuchsia. Selected varieties of fuchsias are at the top of the list for hanging-basket plants in the "fuchsia climates"—the cool, coastal areas. In hot-summer regions, fuchsia enthusiasts must resort to mist spraying to give the plant the climate it needs. Fuchsias will survive a light frost, although leaves and young growth will be injured. In hard-frost areas, treat as an annual, take cuttings for next spring, or bring the entire plant indoors. Spring is the time for pruning: cut back approximately the same amount of growth made the previous summer, or remove frost-injured wood. Fuchsias bloom early and continue through summer to frost. Hang baskets in a location protected from wind and in a partially shaded exposure.

Gardenia (*G. jasminoides* 'Prostrata'). This gardenia grows to 6 or 12 inches high and spreads 2 to 3 feet. Flowers (1 inch) are smaller than the typical gardenia, but have the same fragrance. It needs summer heat for best performance. Grow it in part shade in hot areas, full sun where summers are cooler.

Geranium ivy *(Pelargonium peltatum)*. This attractive vining plant has glossy leaves and numerous round flower clusters of pink, red, white, or lavender. It grows well in full sun in cool climates, but requires partial shade in hot-summer areas. In hard-frost areas, treat it as an annual, or bring the plant indoors and place in a bright window for the winter. 'Sybil Holmes' (pink) and 'Mrs. Banks' (white with purple markings) are popular basket varieties. The plant is hardy to 10°-20°F.

Italian bellflower *(Campanula isophylla)*. This longtime favorite for hanging baskets flowers vigorously in late summer and fall in shades of lavender, blue, and white. Dense foliage hangs down 18 to 24 inches. 'Alba' is a popular white variety; 'Mayi' is a popular blue one.

Ivy *(Hedera helix)*. The trailing habit of this woody vine has made it popular as a container plant both indoors and out. It is available in a wide variety of leaf shapes, sizes, and colors. The small-leaved varieties of 'Baltic ivy', 'Pixie', and 'Needlepoint' are popular for hanging baskets. Don't hesitate to take cuttings from your ivy and grow them in the same pot. Ivy is hardy in all areas.

Juniper. As ground covers, the low-growing junipers grow up to 10 feet wide. Several of the spreading types will spill and drape in hanging baskets. Shore juniper *(Juniperus conferta)* is a natural trailer, adapted to seashore conditions, but it also has good heat tolerance in interior conditions. Bar Harbor juniper *(J. horizontalis)* is fast growing and will spread 10 feet in the open. The grayish-

blue foliage turns plum-colored with cold weather. Andorra juniper *(J. horizontalis* 'Plumosa'*)* is a wide-spreading juniper with a flat-branching habit and gray-green foliage that turns plum in winter. Blue Carpet juniper *(J. horizontalis* 'Wiltonii'*)* is a very low-growing juniper with striking silver-blue color. *Juniper chinensis* 'Nana' has artistic, heavy branches with irregular growth and stubby, dense, blue-green foliage.

Kenilworth ivy *(Cymbalaria muralis).* A perennial vine for hanging in partially shaded locations, its small leaves are somewhat kidney shaped and borne close together along trailing stems. The small flowers are lilac-blue with white and yellow markings; they appear from spring to fall. Commonly, it's grown as an annual in cold-winter areas.

Lantana *(Lantana* species*).* In mild winter areas, this trailing shrub can add year-round color to the container garden. Plants are damaged easily by light frosts, but usually they survive to give a full bloom the following year—just trim out dead wood to maintain a neat appearance. Some of the more colorful cultivars are 'Gold Mound' (yellow-orange), 'Confetti' (pink, yellow, and purple), and 'Carnival' (crimson, lavender, yellow, and pink). Grow lantana in full sun. It is hardy to 20°-24°F.

Moneywort *(Lysimachia nummularia)*—Popular for its foliage as well as its golden-yellow flowers, this hardy perennial can be grown in sun or shade. The trailing stems will produce a cascading display of foliage and flowers in spring and summer. Hardy in all areas.

Parrot's beak *(Lotus berthelotii).* The stems of this finely textured, gray-foliaged plant droop 24 to 36 inches. Small, scarlet flowers appear in abundance in mid-summer. Trim to prevent "legginess" and protect from winter cold. The plant enjoys full sun. It is hardy to 26°-28°F.

Periwinkle, Myrtle *(Vinca major, V. minor).* Commonly and effectively grown as a ground cover, these hardy vines provide an attractive display of draping foliage and 1- to 2-inch blue flowers in the spring. A variegated form of the large-leafed *V. major* is available. There's a white-flower form of the dwarf periwinkle. Of the two, the *V. minor* is the hardier. Both will grow in sun or shade.

Stonecrop *(Sedum seiboldii).* An interesting hanging display is provided by the thick, red-margined leaves and bright pink flowers. Its dense flower clusters provide fall color. Grow it in a sunny location and keep it on the dry side. The plant is completely hardy.

The Shore Juniper (left) and trailing ivy above are good choices for a draping effect.

Almost any flowering plant or vine can adapt to container growing. The colors of the ageratum and yellow calceolaria are complementary.

ANNUALS, PERENNIALS, AND VINES

These plants can give you your own cutting garden and a progression of decorative flower arrangements as they come into flower.

Annuals are those plants that mature, flower, and die all in one season. They are the quickest and easiest way to add color to a garden.

There are many ways to use annuals in containers, and when they are confined to containers, they become moveable flower arrangements. You can place the plants here and there, filling empty spaces as needed with the bright colors of pansies or petunias. You can also use them to highlight other plants or garden features or to call attention to a doorway. For instance, white impatiens can help liven up a shady corner, and the bright colors of marigolds or zinnias make an entryway much more inviting.

Perennials are those plants that come back year after year. The term *perennial* is used by most gardeners to refer to flowering plants. It is often used as a catch-all term for anything that does not complete its life cycle in one year.

Practically speaking, of course, climate can determine what is *annual* and what is *perennial*. In mild regions of the West and South, tender plants such as geraniums and chrysanthemums can live year after year. In colder regions, however, these plants would be treated as annuals.

In containers, your favorite perennials can be moved into view when they are at their showy best and out of view when they become dormant. Or, they can be mixed with annuals for a longer show.

Vines can be annual or perennial, deciduous or evergreen. Their growth habit makes them ideal for container growing, and keeping vines confined offers the advantage of easy control of the fast-growing varieties.

When choosing a vine, you should first know what kind of support it will need. Clinging vines such as English ivy can attach to anything. Vines that twine can climb a single wire or pole. However, vines with tendrils need support across as well as up and down.

There are many plants that will perform well within the confines of a container. You'll find an extensive list on the following pages. All the plants listed here meet two basic conditions: they are generally available, and they are worthy of special attention. However, this list is not exhaustive; treat the entries as suggestions only. All available plants should be considered for their container or hanging-basket potential. There is an additional list on pages 46-49 of bulbs, vines, ground covers, and shrubs that are good in hanging baskets.

The following chart of annuals, and perennials used as annuals, indicates the plant's best use. When that use is "hanging baskets," you can feature the plant alone; "hanging bouquets" means tuck the plants into the basket or column.

The second column tells whether the plant is a cool- or warm-season performer. Cool-season performers are generally frost tolerant and will go to seed quickly during summer's long, warm days. Warm-season plants, however, need the long, warm days of summer to develop and flower fully. The warm-season annuals generally are killed by the first heavy frost in fall.

You can grow any of these plants from seed or from transplants. Transplants are a safer bet where the germination period is long (check column 7).

Ageratum

Alyssum 'Rosie O'Day' and pansies.

Red begonias with alyssum, marigolds, and ivy.

Name	Warm- or Cool-Season Plant	Season of Bloom	Size and Form	Color	Exposure* S	PS	FS	Days to Germination	Sowing to flowering (weeks)	Comments	Uses
Ageratum	W	S, F	6-12" mounds	Shades of blue, purple most useful	•	•		8	12	Can be brought indoors in fall for winter bloom.	Hanging bouquet tuck-in. Or plant 3 or 4 in shallow box. Combine with marigolds or pink petunias
'Blue Blazer'			6"	Deep blue						Compact; flowers profusely.	
'Blue Jay'			4"	Light blue						More uniform and compact than above.	
'Blue Mink'			12"	Light blue						More vigorous than above. Large flower heads.	
'Blue Puffs' ('Blue Danube')			7"	Light blue						Very uniform plants.	
'Summer Snow'			6"	White						Similar plant form as 'Blue Blazer'.	
Alyssum	C-W	Sp, S, F	3-8" low trailing mat	White, purple, and rose	•	•		8	8	Fast-growing, tough plant. Profuse bloomer. Faintly fragrant. Will spread 10-15".	Low growing. 'Tiny Tim' most useful in hanging bouquets. A most versatile plant. Use as ground cover in tubbed shrub or tree.
'Carpet of Snow'			4"	White						Forms very dense carpet of flowers.	
'Tiny Tim'			2-3"	White						Early flowering miniature.	
'Rosie O'Day' (AAS)			4"	Deep rose						Retains deep color well.	
'Royal Carpet' (AAS)			3-5"	Violet-purple						Profuse flowers.	
'Oriental Night'			4"	Dark purple						Compact plants similar to 'Tiny Tim'.	
'Pastel Carpet'			3-4"	Wide range						Unusual color effect.	

*S = sun; PS = part shade; FS = full shade; AAS = All American Selection

White alyssum and dwarf marigolds.

Fibrous begonias in a hanging basket.

Name	Warm- or Cool-Season Plant	Season of Bloom	Size and Form	Color	Exposure* S	PS	FS	Days to Germination	Sowing to flowering (weeks)	Comments	Uses
Bachelor's Button	C-W	Sp, S	10-36" erect, bushy	Blue, red, pink, and white shades	•	•		10	10	Scorched early by summer heat.	Dwarf forms best for pots. Favored as cut flowers and old-time boutonnieres.
'Jubilee Gem'			12"	Deep blue						Neat bushy habit. Good blue color.	
'Polka Dot Mix'			15"	Blue, red, pink, and white						Good habit. Silvery foliage with ruffled flowers.	
'Snowball' (AAS)			12"	White						Heat resistant. Long bloom period.	
Balsam	W	S, F	8-30" erect	Wide range: pink to purple, rose shades, scarlet, and white		•		8	12	Takes full sun in cool areas. Camellia and bush types best for containers.	Hanging bouquets combine with the earliest-to-bloom annuals.
'Tom Thumb'			10"	Color mix						Very compact habit. Profuse bloomer.	
Camellia-flowered			15"	Color mix						Extra-double blooms.	
Begonia, fibrous	C-W	S, F	6-14" erect, bushy	Red, rose, pink shades, and white	•	•	•	14-21	16	Green foliage varieties will develop bronze color in full sun. Bright window provides indoor winter bloom. See Begonia variety chart.	Hanging bouquets. Hanging columns. Combine 'Viva' and 'Scarletta' for a red-and-white living bouquet.
Browallia	C-W	S, F	8-18" spreading	Blue shades, and white		•		15	12	Blooms profusely.	Hanging baskets. One of the few brilliant blue flowers. Excellent cut flower. In fall, cut back and pot up for winter bloom indoors.
'Blue Bells Improved'			8-10"	Lavender-blue						Base-branching, needs no pinching. Neat and compact habit.	
'Silver Bells'			8-10"	White						Same fine habit as above.	
'Sky Bells'			8-10"	Powder blue						Good habit. Large flowers.	

*S = sun; PS = part shade; FS = full shade; AAS = All American Selection

White candytuft with English daisies and ageratum.

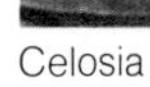

Celosia

Coleus

Name	Warm- or Cool-Season Plant	Season of Bloom	Size and Form	Color	Exposure* S	PS	FS	Days to Germination	Sowing to flowering (weeks)	Comments	Uses
Calendula	C-W	Sp, S	6-24″ compact, spreading	Orange, yellow shades, and cream	•	•		10	8	Best in cool temperatures. Blooms in winter in mild areas. Earliest color in spring, from fall transplanting.	Plant for late-winter color in pots, boxes, or tubs. Will take sharp frosts.
'Pacific Beauty'			18″	Many shades of above colors						Heat resistant. Long-stemmed flowers are great for cutting.	
'Coronets'			12″	Orange, yellow						Heat-resistant dwarf.	
Candytuft (Annual *Iberis*)	C-W	Sp, S	6-15″ mounds	Red, pink, lavender, purple, shades, and white	•	•		8	10	Best in cool-summer areas. Hyacinth flowering type is less hardy, not as good in pots. Sow 2-3 weeks apart for continuous bloom.	Pots, window boxes. Dwarf hybrids best in hanging bouquets. Hyacinth flowering type makes good cut flowers.
'Umbellata Dwarf Fairy'			8″	Many shades of above						Very compact plants. Somewhat heat resistant.	
Celosia	W	S, F	6-36″ erect	Yellow, gold, purple, pink, and red shades	•			10	8	Dwarf varieties best for containers. Many bright-colored varieties available. Cold sensitive.	Plant the plumes in a box next to carrots.
Plumosa Type 'Fairy Fountains'			14″	Color mix						Good base-branching habit. Vigorous grower with long bloom.	
'Fiery Feather'			12″	Red						Uniform pyramid-shaped plumes.	
Cockscomb Type 'Jewel Box'			4-8″	Color mix						Compact miniature plants covered with large combs.	
Coleus	W		12-30″ erect	Wide variety of foliage color combinations in red, pink, green, and yellow		•	•	10		8-10 weeks from sowing to mature size. Direct filtered light is best indoors. Pinch tips to encourage branching. Many different leaf forms.	Grown for spectacular leaf color. Pot for light shade outdoors, indirect light indoors.
'Carefree'			12″	Available as mix or separate colors						Self-branching. Needs no pinching to maintain excellent habit. Small, closely spaced leaves.	
'Rainbow'			15″	Available as mix or separate colors						More vigorous and larger-leaved than above; needs pinching. Fringed or finely serrated leaves.	
'Sabre' series			16″	Mixed colors						Compact habit. Base-branching. "Willow-like" leaves.	

*S = sun; PS = part shade; FS = full shade; AAS = All American Selection

Dianthus with Irish moss.

Gazania

Geranium 'Sprinter'

Name	Warm- or Cool-Season Plant	Season of Bloom	Size and Form	Color	Exposure* S	Exposure* PS	Exposure* FS	Days to Germination	Sowing to flowering (weeks)	Comments	Uses
Dianthus	C-W	Sp, S, F	3-15" erect, bushy	White, pink, salmon, red, rose, and violet	•	•		7	6-12	Lacy blue-grey foliage. Takes afternoon shade in hot areas. Fragrant flowers.	Dwarf varieties best in pots. Try 'Wee Willie' in an early season hanging bouquet, combined with strawberries.
'Baby Doll'			8"	Vivid shades of red, pink, violet, and white					6-8	Sturdy and compact plant. Plain-edged single flowers.	
'China Doll' (AAS)			10-12"	Pink, red, and salmon shades edged white					10-12	Compact, base-branching. Double flowers in clusters.	
'Magic Charms' (AAS)			6"	White, rose, scarlet, and pink shades					6-8	Excellent base-branching; compact habit. fringed, single blossoms, some speckled.	
'Queen of Hearts' (AAS)			15"	Brilliant scarlet-red					12-15	Compact, base-branching; vigorous habit. Single flowers.	
'Wee Willie'			3" compact mound	Red, rose shades, and white					6-8	Long-blooming, sweet-scented, single flowers. Very compact plants.	
Gazania 'Sunshine Mix'	W	S, F	8" erect	Cream, yellow, orange, pink, bronze, and red, some with contrasting zones	•			10	10	Thrives in hot, dry areas. Large, brightly colored, 5", daisy-like, long-blooming flowers, many with contrasting centers.	Colorful in large pots and boxes. Blooms until frost.
Geranium (from seed)	W	S, F	18-24" erect,	Red, scarlet, pink, rose, pink shades, and salmon	•	•		14-21	16		A long-standing favorite for containers indoors and outdoors.
'Carefree'			24" erect with basal branching	Separate colors or mix						See text (page 00).	
'Sprinter'			18" erect							More dwarfed than 'Carefree', and earlier flowering.	
Impatiens	W	S, F	10-20" mounds	Solid and bicolored shades of red, pink, violet, orange, and white		•	•	18	12	Blooms profusely. See impatiens chart for varieties. A bright window will provide indoor winter bloom.	In pots, tubs, hanging baskets, or hanging bouquets. Solves problem of color in the shade.

*S = sun; PS = part shade; FS = full shade; AAS = All American Selection

Marigold

Nasturtium

Nemesia

Name	Warm- or Cool-Season Plant	Season of Bloom	Size and Form	Color	Exposure* S	PS	FS	Days to Germination	Sowing to flowering (weeks)	Comments	Uses
Lobelia	C-W	S, F	5-18" trailing or erect	Lavender-blue, pink, white	•	•		18	18	Shearing after first flowering may provide second bloom. Slow from seed. Blooms profusely.	Plant trailing types in hanging baskets or at base of shrubs in boxes. Plant erect types in pots and boxes.
'Crystal Palace'			5" erect	Dark blue						Dark bronze-green foliage.	
'Mrs. Clibran' ('Bright Eyes')			5" erect	Violet-blue with white centers						Medium-green foliage.	
'Blue Cascade'			18" trailing	Light blue						Green foliage. Large flowers.	
'Sapphire'			18" trailing	Dark blue with white centers						Light green foliage.	
Marigolds	C-W	S, F	6-36" erect or bushy	Yellow, gold, red, and orange shades, solid and bicolors	•			7	8-14	Sizes available for every container. See Marigold chart for varieties. Easy care. Profuse bloomer.	Dwarf varieties in hanging bouquets. Taller varieties good as cut flowers.
Nasturtium	C-W	Sp, S, F	12-15" bushy or 24" trailing vine	Maroon, red, orange, rose, yellow, and cream, solid and bicolors	•			10	6	Best for cool climates. Leaves, seeds, and flowers are edible. Profuse bloomers. Prefers dry soil.	Quick color in pots and hanging baskets. Good cut flowers.
'Dwarf Double Jewel'			12" bushy	Rose, mahogany, yellow, and orange-scarlet						Compact habit. Double flowers held above foliage.	
'Double Gleam' (AAS)			24" trailing	Complete nasturtium range						Large, sweet-scented flowers, double and semi-double.	
Nemesia	C	Sp, S	8-24" erect	All colors but green	•			10	12	Lacks heat tolerance. 'Nana Compacta' (10") dwarf varieties are best for containers.	Charming in hanging bouquet, pots, and window boxes. Pinch to make bushy.
'Carnival Blend'			10"	White, red, orange, and yellow						Compact, base-branching plant.	
Nicotiana	W	S, F	8-36" erect or bushy	Red, rose, lavender, green shades, and white	•	•		15	8-10	Prefers afternoon shade in hot areas. Fragrant. Most flowers open in early morning and at dusk.	Excellent in pots. Good for cut flowers.
'White Bedder'			15" bushy	White						Profuse bloom. Compact, sturdy plants.	
'Crimson Bedder'			18" bushy	Crimson						Same as above.	
'Nicki' series			18"	Pink, rose, and white						Self-branching, and compact. Free-flowering.	

*S = sun; PS = part shade; FS = full shade; AAS = All American Selection

Nicotiana

Pansy

Petunias

Name	Warm- or Cool-Season Plant	Season of Bloom	Size and Form	Color	Exposure* S	PS	FS	Days to Germination	Sowing to flowering (weeks)	Comments	Uses
Nierembergia	C-W	S, F	6-10" mat	Violet-blue	•	•		15	16	Compact, densely branched, slightly spreading plant. Perennial in mild-winter areas. Profuse bloom.	Pots and hanging baskets.
'Purple Robe'			6"	Violet-blue						Forms dense mat covered with flowers.	
Pansy	C	Sp, S, F	6-8" erect	Full range, some blotched	•	•		10		Winter bloom from summer sowing, in mild areas. Primarily spring bloom in hot-summer areas. All varieties suited for containers.	Hanging bouquets in mixed colors. Many uses in pots, window boxes, and planters.
'Imperial Blue' (AAS)			7"	Light blue with violet face, gold eye						Heat resistant. Long bloom. Large flowers.	
'Majestic Giants' (AAS)			6"	Wide range, blotched						Large 4" flowers. Blooms through summer.	
Petunias	W	Sp, S, F	12-15" bushy mounds	Wide range, red, pink, blue, purple, yellow, orange, white, single and bicolored shades	•			12	12-15	Very versatile. All do well in containers. F-1 hybrids are best performers. Choose variety for color and flower form, single or double, ruffled or plain-edged.	Versatile. All uses: containers, hanging baskts, and hanging bouquets.
Grandiflora varieties										Greatest vigor. Ruffled large flowers but not as prolific-flowering as multifloras.	
Multiflora varieties										More compact and uniform than grandifloras. Best weather resistance. Smaller flowers than above but greater total bloom. Plain-edged flowers.	
Phlox, annual	C-W	S, F	6-15" erect or bushy	Blue, violet crimson, pink, yellow, white, shades	•			12	10	Some varieties are heat sensitive. Transplanting is difficult. Small seedlings often flower best.	Grow in pots and hanging bouquets. Makes fine cut flowers.
'Dwarf Beauty Mix'			6-7"							Compact plant. Profuse bloom.	
'Globe Mix'			8"							Base-branching, ball-shaped plants. Heat resistant. Large flowers.	
'Twinkle Mix' (AAS)			7"							Star-patterned flowers fringed with pointed petals.	

*S = sun; PS = part shade; FS = full shade; AAS = All American Selection

Primula malacoides

Red salvia

Dwarf snapdragon

Name	Warm- or Cool-Season Plant	Season of Bloom	Size and Form	Color	Exposure* S	PS	FS	Days to Germination	Sowing to flowering (weeks)	Comments	Uses
Portulaca	W	S, F	6" trailing	Red, pink, rose, lavender, yellow, white and red	•			10	8	Thrives in hot dry locations; prolific flowering.	In shallow pots and containers, hanging baskets.
'Sunglo' series				Individual or mixed colors							
Primula	C	W, Sp, F	5-20"	Red, pink, rose, lavender, purple, blue and white shades	•	•		5-8 (mos. seed to flower)	21-28	Not heat tolerant. Spring and fall use in cold-winter areas. Many species available.	Edge, pots, hanging bouquet.
P. malacoides			5-15"							Look for 'Rhinepearl' series.	
P. obconica			8-15"							Long bloom period.	
P. polyanthus			12"							Brilliant colors, including yellow and orange.	
Salvia	W	S, F	6-30" erect and bushy	Scarlet-red. white, pink, and blue	•	•		12-15	8-10	Grown for its bright red flower spikes. Dwarf forms are best for containers. Will not tolerate full shade or cold.	Grow in large pots and boxes. Cool down its strong color with white petunias.
'Scarlet Pygmy'			6"	Scarlet						Early flowering on compact, rounded plants.	
'Hot Jazz'			14"	Dark scarlet-red						Large, dark green leaves. Tightly flowered spike.	
'St. John's Fire'			12"	Scarlet-red						Early, heavy bloom on a small, compact plant.	
Snapdragon	C-W	Sp, S, F	6-36"	Many red, pink, rose, orange, yellow, bronze, lavender, shades, and white	•			7-14	14	Dwarf forms best in containers. In mild-winter areas, a late-summer sowing produces winter bloom. Cut back spikes after flowering for continuous bloom.	Dwarf types give good show in planters. Tallest varieties may be too tall for container growing, but make good cut flowers.
'Floral Carpet'			7"	Many of above						Mound-shaped plants produce many 3" spikes. Long bloom.	
'Little Darling' (AAS)			15"	Many of above						Open flowers (snapless). Compact, base-branching plants with profuse bloom.	
Sweet Peas	C-W	Sp, S	8-36" mounds or climbing vine	White, red, pink, blue, lavender shades, and white	•			15	16	Small bush types best for containers. Profuse bloomers. Generally heat sensitive. Winter bloom in mild areas.	Grow in large pots and tubs. Good cut flowers.
'Bijou'			15" bush type	All of above						Early, heat-resistant plant covered with long-stemmed, ruffled flowers.	
'Knee Hi'			30" will climb	All of above						Compact. Heat resistant. Large flowers.	
'Little Sweetheart'			8" bush type	All of above						Compact, bushy mounds covered with ruffled flowers	

*S = sun; PS = part shade; FS = full shade; AAS = All American Selection

Zinnia bed

Verbena

Name	Warm- or Coo Season Plant	Season of Bloom	Size and Form	Color	Exposure* S	PS	FS	Days to Germination	Sowing to flowering (weeks)	Comments	Uses
Thunbergia	W	S, F	Trailing vine	Orange, yellow white with black throat	•			12	12-16	Dense foliage. Profuse blooms. Will overwinter in mild areas.	Trailers for hanging baskets.
T. alata (Black-eyed Susan vine)				All of above						Flowers 1″ wide.	
T. gibsonii 'Orange Lantern'				Orange with black throat						Flowers 2″ wide.	
Torenia	W	S, F	8″ mounds	White or violet-blue with golden-yellow throat		•		15	12-16	Compact bushy plants. *T. Fournieri* 'Compacta' is the available form.	Use in pots and window boxes. Combine with lobelia, small ferns.
Verbena	C-W	S, F	4-20″ spreading mounds	Red, pink, blue, purple, and white shades, some with white centers	•			20	10-12	Compact bush type best for containers. Drought tolerant. Profuse bloomer in hot climates.	A native American plant with about the truest red, white, and blue colors available in bedding plants. Vibrant clusters of flowers stand out in pots, window boxes, or hanging baskets. Needs full sun.
'Blaze' (AAS)			8″	Scarlet						Excellent compact habit. Dark green foliage. Large flowers.	
'Amethyst' (AAS)			8″	Blue						Same fine habit as above.	
'Sparkle Mix'			8″	All colors, mostly with white centers						Same plant form as 'Amethyst' and 'Blaze'.	
'Rainbow Mix'			8″	Mixed, most with white centers						More upright than others. Ideal for pots.	
Vinca (Periwinkle) *Catharanthus roseus* Madagascar periwinkle	W	S, F		Red, pink, rise, and white with contrasting center	•	•		15	12-14		This is the annual vinca, not to be confused with the perennial ground cover (*Vinca major, V. minor*). Bright, phlox-like flowers stand out against glossy foliage. Best in pots and boxes.
Dwarf Type			10″							Compact habit; includes 'Little Blanche', 'Little Bright Eye', 'Little Pinkie', and 'Little Delicate'.	
'Polka Dot' (AAS)			6″ trailing	White with red center							
Zinnia	W	S, F	6-30″ erect	Wide range of solid and bicolors	•			7	8	Many sizes and flower forms. Best in heat	Taller varieties can be massed in large containers for showy display and cut flowers. Shorter bushier varieties are excellent for potted color in full, hot sun.
'Buttons' (AAS)			10″	Pink, red, and yellow shades						Compact habit. Covered with double flowers.	
'Peter Pan' (AAS)			12″	Orange, scarlet, rose, pink, and cream						Compact. Large double flowers are impressive in pots.	
'Thumbelina' (AAS)			6″	Complete range						Double flowers appear when plants are only 4″ tall. Long blooming season.	

*S = sun; PS = part shade; FS = full shade; AAS = All American Selection

The fibrous begonia 'Glamour'

What's New and Colorful?

An annual pageant of color appears in all phases of the garden world—first in the great seed farms; then in the nursery greenhouses; then in the seed catalogs; and finally in pots, boxes, and borders. In this ritual of renewal, "new plants" and "new colors" and forms of old plants are selected and scientifically engineered. This book pays tribute to all members of the pageant, with special attention to recent eyecatchers.

The judgments, though made carefully, are not permanent. A new introduction may hold its popularity for many years or only a few months.

For a no-nonsense way to determine whether the new varieties will grow in *your* garden as advertised, try a few comparative plantings (the small scale offered by boxes and pots makes such experiments easy enough). Try out one or two plants of a new variety, or even of an older variety you've never yet attempted, and compare them with your usual variety. Plants marked AAS (All-America Selection) have already been tested and should do well in any part of the country.

Begonias. 'Glamour'—An addition to the large-flowered, fibrous-rooted begonias. The flowers, larger than those of any other varieties in its class, appear when the plants are only 3 inches high. In a test garden, the compact growth habit, prolific flowering, and glossy, waxy foliage made 'Glamour' a favorite. If grown in the flowerbed it will reach 10 inches high, but in a pot it will stay a compact 6 to 8 inches. Plants (unpinched) can still be compact in 4-inch pots after four months of growth. 'Glamour' begonias have excellent heat tolerance—logically enough, considering that they were developed in Florida.

Fibrous Begonias—New and Old

Variety	Color	Comment
Dwarf (6-8")		
'Linda'	Deep rose	Very free-flowering, compact, and weather resistant.
'Viva'	Pure white	
'Scarletta'	Scarlet-red	Excellent habit, darker foliage than above.
'White Tausendschon'	White	Compact; early, profuse bloom.
'Derby'	White-edged, salmon	Uniform, compact, and early.
'Comets'	Red, rose, pink, white, and 'Galaxy Mix'	Bronze foliage; compact all season; white may be taller.
Cocktail Mix	'Gin'—pink, 'Vodka'—scarlet-red, 'Whiskey'—white	Bronze foliage; compact and sun resistant.
'Electra'	Light scarlet-tinged salmon	Weather resistant and early.
Intermediate (8-12")		
'Pink Tausendschon'	Pink	Very free-flowering.
'Red Tausendschon'	Red	Bronze-green foliage; free-flowering.
'Organdy' Mix	Red, rose, and pink	20% bronze foliage; soft colors.
'Othello'	Scarlet-orange	Bronze foliage; good in pots or in the garden.
'Glamour'	Red, pink, and rose	Green foliage.
Tall (12-14")		
Caravelle Series	Red, rose, and pink	Well-shaped, large leaves must be pinched.
'Fortuna'	Rose, scarlet	Large-flowered and bushy; taller than above.
'Danica'	Rose, scarlet	Similar to 'Fortuna' but has bronze foliage.
'Cinderella'	Rose, white, with yellow center	50% large and 50% small flowers.

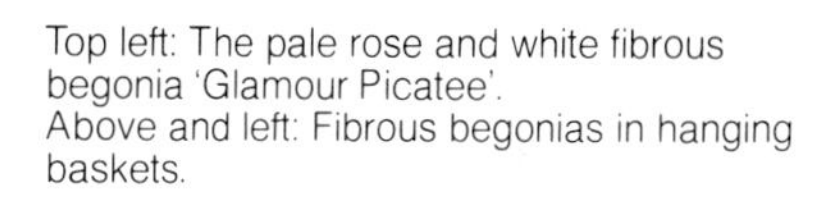

Top left: The pale rose and white fibrous begonia 'Glamour Picatee'.
Above and left: Fibrous begonias in hanging baskets.

Carnations. 'Juliet'—Grown in test gardens across the country, the performance of this variety merited an award from the All-America Selection Committee. The flowers are fully double, measuring 2½ inches in diameter, with a bright scarlet-red color. Their uniformity in trial grounds is most impressive—they all seem to be exactly 12 inches high. Try this compact carnation massed in a large container.

Dahlias. The dahlia enthusiast may look scornfully upon the quick-growing dahlia from seed, but many changes have occurred since the days of 'Unwin Dwarf' seed dahlias. Plant breeders now offer many colorful, compact varieties.

'Rigoletto'—This variety has generated enthusiasm among commercial growers: it is early (one week earlier than 'Early Bird'), and its habit is compact. Another major attraction is that it has more double flowers than any other existing variety. The brightly colored flowers are produced on 15-inch-tall, well-branched plants. When grown in pots, 'Rigoletto' will maintain a compact 12-inch-tall habit.

Geraniums. A bushy red geranium in a moss-covered pot seems to embody home gardening to most people. Perhaps it's because geraniums have been popular in homes and gardens since before the American Revolution, and even now many people get their first gardening pleasure from growing geraniums. Although the plant and flower have undergone many changes through breeding and have been greatly improved, still the geranium retains its old-fashioned quality. Versatility and a failure-proof reputation have always been its big appeal.

In recent years, geranium breeders finally have perfected strains that grow "true" from seed. And since geraniums are as easy to grow from seed as from cuttings, you might as well plant seed so that you can have geranium annuals in the spring and summer garden. Most varieties require about 120 days from seed to first bloom, so start seed indoors in February for a mid-July bloom. They will bloom freely outdoors until frost; at that point, pot them up and bring them indoors for winter color.

The seed-grown varieties outdo the cutting varieties for their bushy habit and long flowering period. Among the seed geraniums, some of the leading varieties are the Carefree series and the Sprinter series. The latter now includes 'Sprinter Deep Red', 'Sprinter Salmon', and 'Sprinter White'.

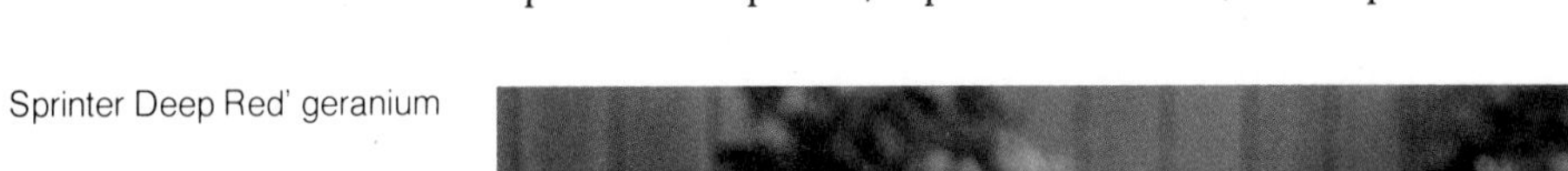

Sprinter Deep Red' geranium

Impatiens. Shade-lovers that add color to areas shunned by other annuals, impatiens look magnificent in hanging baskets as well as in other containers. They will tolerate dry conditions and low soil-fertility. Varieties come in a wide range of colors and plant heights. Some unique additions are the following varieties:

'Fancifrills'—Available only as plants, this unusual variety offers brightly colored, double flowers on 15-inch-tall plants. Their well-formed buds resemble small rosebuds. They can be grown in a 4- or 5-inch pot, if pinched regularly to stimulate branching. They provide a colorful display in the flowerbed.

'Twinkles'—This variegated flowered impatiens has a red and white bicolor pattern that's more distinct than that of most other variegated varieties. Its compact plant habit makes it adapt well to pots and baskets as well as flowerbeds.

'Futura'—Compact plants produce brightly colored, large flowers that provide a striking color display in the flowerbed or in a hanging basket (see photo).

Many varieties of impatiens are best displayed in containers and hanging baskets.

Impatiens Varieties

Variety	Color	Comment
Dwarf Single Color (6-10")		
Elfin Series	Pink, white, orange, salmon, rose, red, mix	Basal branching; no pinching needed; very dwarf; free-flowering; large, early bloom.
Gem Series	Orange, pink salmon, rose scarlet, violet, and white	1½" flowers on compact plants, similar to 'Futura'.
Dwarf Bicolors (6-10")		
'General Guisan' ('A-Go-Go')	Scarlet red and white	Neat habit; deep green foliage; hybrid has better form than inbred.
'Stars and Stripes'	Scarlet, rose, pink, crimson, orange, salmon, bicolored, white	Good dwarf habit; bronze foliage; flowers blotched or striped white.
'Zig-Zag'	Rose, scarlet, salmon, pink, orange, bicolored white	Similar to impatiens in habit.
Semi-Dwarf Single Colors (12-15")		
Grande Mix	Wide range	'Elfin'-like habit; dwarfer than other large-flowered forms.
Imp Series	Carmine, pink, orange, purple, rose, scarlet, white, salmon, mix	Uniform, well-branched habit; large flowers, hardy; good in difficult shaded area.
Minette Series	Orange, salmon, rose, pink, white, scarlet, mix	Basal branching; no pinching needed; Elfin bloom with more vigor.
'Tangeglow'	Bright orange	Free-flowering; dark, glossy foliage; large flowers with rich color.
Semi-Dwarf Bicolors (12-15")		
Ripple Series	Rose, scarlet, orange, fuchsia, bicolored white	Good dwarf branching habit; large bloom; clear star pattern.

Even a small display of marigolds can be impressive.

Marigold Height and Form

Surprisingly, the marigolds grown in test gardens grew to the height listed in nursery catalogs. All the tall varieties grew taller than the catalogs indicated.

Variety	Height	Flower	Coment
'Petite Gold'*	6"	Fully double 1¼" golden flowers on compact mounds	Petite series; French type; including 'Petite Orange' AAS, 'Petite Yellow', and 'Petite Mix'.
'Petite Spry'	7"	Double red with yellow crest	
'Petite Harmony'*	8"	Mahogany red and orange	
'Pigmy Primrose'	7"	Primrose yellow with red	Early flowering, French type; 'Red Pygmy' also.
'Brownie Scout'	8"	Fully double 1¼"; gold splashed with red	French type with 'petite' mound habit.
'Yellow Nugget'	10-12"	Double 2¼" flowers; triploid	Nugget series also includes; 'Orange Nugget', 'Gold Nugget', and mixed colors.
'Pumpkin Crush'	10-12"	Huge, fully double 4½" orange blooms	Guys and Dolls series also offered as yellow, gold, and mixed varieties.
'Aztec'	10-12"	Gold, yellow orange, mix 3-4" flowers	Double-carnation type.
'Bolero'*	10-12"	Fully double 2½" flowers; bright maroon, gold center	Double French bicolor.
'Honeycomb'	10-12"	Fully double 1½" crested blooms; maroon petals, gold border	Royal Crested series also includes the bicolors 'Autumn Haze', 'Gold Rush', and 'Star Dust'.
'Gold Cupid'	10-12"	Mum-like 2½" blooms	Cupid series includes orange, yellow, and mix varieties.
'Spanish Brocade'	10-12"	Gold and deep red blooms	Sparky-type French bicolors; very early
'Fiesta'	12"	Carnation-type crimson and yellow	Olé series includes 'Matador' and 'Picador'.
'Tiger'	12-15"	Closely packed petals of bright gold	Triploid hybrid with extra long flowering period; earliest of the group.
'Showboat'*	13"	2½" golden yellow	Triploid hybrid; group includes 'Gold Bullion'.
'Apollo'	14"	Golden-orange 3" double blooms	'Space Age' series includes 'Moonshot' and 'Space Age' mixture.
'Harvest Moon'	14"	Crested 1½" orange blooms	Moon series also includes 'Honey', and 'Honey Moon' (yellow); blooms at 6".
'Rusty Red'	14"	Well-doubled 2½" rusty mahogany	Becomes marked with gold as it matures.
'Gold Galore'*	14-16"	Double-carnation-type 3¼" golden yellow	Compact 'Galore' series includes 'Yellow' and 'Orange'.
'First Lady'*	18"	Double-carnation-type 3¼" yellow	Lady series includes 'Gold Lady' and 'Orange Lady'; hedge type; erect, bushy, rounded.
'Naughty Marietta'	18-20"	2" single golden yellow with red eye	Also lower-growing 'Cinnabar' and 'Dainty Marietta'.
'Senator Dirksen'	24"	Double-carnation-type 3½" golden yellow	Hedge type; very vigorous.
'Orange Hawaii'	30-36"	Double-carnation-type 4" blooms	Odorless foliage; carnation flowered; series includes 'Golden Hawaii'.
'Yellow Crackerjack'	30-36"	Double-carnation-type 5" blooms	Crackerjack series; also offered as orange, gold, and mix; erect, bushy.
'Yellow Doubloon'	36"	Extra double 3½-4" carnation-type blooms	Gold Coin series includes: 'Sovereign' (gold), and 'Double Eagle' (orange).

*AAS

Marigolds. It's difficult to improve on the foolproof performance of the existing marigold varieties, but some worthy contributions have been made in the triploid hybrid group. Their performance is impressive; they stand up to intense summer heat and heavy rains. Here are a few additions to the chart in the triploid hybrid class:

'Legal Gold'—Prolific flowering on stocky 12-inch-tall plants. The gold flowers are double, with a 2½-inch diameter. This is an excellent pot plant.

'Red Nugget'—A red-flowered addition to the existing 'Nugget' series. The flowers are double, 2 inches in diameter, and are produced on compact plants that grow only 10 inches tall in pots.

Snapdragons. 'Pixie Mix'—This dwarf snapdragon is in the "open flower class" (snapless) and offers a color blend of orange, pink, red, white, and yellow flowers. In the garden it will reach a height of 6 to 8 inches. This plant is excellent for growing in 4-inch pots.

Zinnias. 'Pink Ruffles'—This zinnia makes an excellent companion to 'Scarlet Ruffles', which received an All-America gold medal. The double pink flowers are produced on well-branched 24- to 30-inch plants. A major characteristic of these varieties is their long stems, which makes them superb for cut flowers. Both these varieties have grown in various trial grounds; their excellent flower form and prolific flowering are impressive. If you have a place for a large tub or box, 'Pink Ruffles' makes an interesting container choice.

'Pixie Pink' snapdragon.

A truly serviceable flower, the marigold can also be used in hanging baskets.

The lavender blossoms of this wisteria create a feeling of coolness near a pool. Wisteria is a vine that can be trained as a small tree.

SHRUBS AND TREES IN CONTAINERS

Container growing enables you to control the growth of plants more easily.

There's nothing modern about growing trees and shrubs in boxes. About 3,500 years ago, commercial nurserymen brought Frankincense trees in containers from the Somali Coast to Egypt. And as far back as 4,000 years ago, the Egyptians grew trees in large "boxes" or "pots" cut into rock and filled with special soil.

These days, you can walk through a nursery and find countless plants that do well in containers. However, *all* plants—at least in their youthful stages—can be grown in containers. And since you can control and discipline the growth of containerized plants, it makes sense to plant slow-growing shrubs and trees; they will accept container conditions for years.

Shrubs For Containers

The following shrubs and trees are suitable for container growing.

Althea *(Hibiscus syriacus)*. Deciduous. This widely used member of the Hibiscus family blooms in an array of either single or double flowers (2½ to 3 inches) in summer. Foliage is bright green, unevenly toothed, and sometimes lobed. Erect and compact when young, it requires more pruning to shape when older. In winter, partially prune last year's growth for larger flowers the following summer. It does well in partial shade or full sun and is hardy in all areas.

Chinese Hibiscus *(H. rosa-sinensis)*. Evergreen. Yielding lavish summer color, this plant sports large (4 to 8 inches), showy, single or double flowers in many colors, with glossy leaves. Choose among many varieties for flower color and plant habit. Warm weather and sun will promote the best bloom; it needs afternoon shade in hottest areas. Since it is cold sensitive (hardy to 20°F. with overhead protection), bring it indoors in cold-winter areas.

Cleyera *(Cleyera japonica)*. Evergreen. This slow-growing shrub (6 to 8 feet) has colorful foliage on gracefully arching branches. New, brownish-red leaves gradually turn lustrous deep green, retaining a red midrib. Small clusters of fragrant white flowers bloom in spring, followed by dark-red berries lasting into winter. Grow as you would its relative, the camellia (see page 47). The plant is hardy to 0°F.

English Lavender *(Lavandula angustifolia)*. Evergreen. Highly valued for its fragrance, this small (12- to 48-inch) shrub is a pleasant addition to any patio. Strongly fragrant purple to lavender flowers are borne on long (18- to 24-inch) spikes in midsummer. Its gray foliage is aromatic. Prune after flowering to maintain compactness. It is hardy in all areas.

Euonymus *(E. fortunei)*. Evergreen. Finely textured foliage and varied forms make the euonymus a valued container plant. One that deserves special attention is 'Emerald Cushion', with a dense, compact, mounded habit, and rich green foliage. 'Sarcoxie', an equally dense but more erect variety, takes well to shear-

ing, makes an excellent espalier, and is ideal for low planter boxes. If given a wall or trellis to climb, *E. fortunei* variety *radicans* will cover it completely with thick green leaves. For a graceful traced or outline effect, try 'Kewensis', which has smaller leaves. Grow it in full sun or partial shade. The plant is hardy in all areas.

A gardenia trained as a standard.

Flowering Quince *(Chaenomeles* species*)*. Deciduous. For the earliest spring excitement, the flowering quince deserves center stage among the shrubs. It is one of the earliest spring bloomers, and its flowers come in shades of white, red, and pink. Leafless branches and flowers have an appealing oriental feel. Leaves are tinged red when young, then gradually turn lustrous green. This shrub is easily pruned to shape or espalier and requires little care. It is hardy in all areas.

Gardenia *(G. jasminoides)*. Evergreen. The gardenia's special style is accented when it's grown in containers and placed up front in entryways, decks, or patios. The waxy, white flowers are beautifully fragrant, especially in the evening. Leaves are glossy green. It blooms from late spring into summer, and occasionally throughout the year, in mild climates. It grows best in filtered shade, but will take full sun if given ample moisture. The plant requires summer heat for the best bloom. It is hardy to 20°F.

Glossy Abelia *(A. × grandiflora)*. Evergreen to semi-deciduous. Offering a colorful combination of foliage and flowers, it has coppery new leaves that gradually turn glossy green, as well as arching branches. Flower clusters bloom white to pinkish-white from early summer into fall. Prune selectively in late winter. For the best color, grow it in full sun. It is hardy to 0°F.

Heavenly Bamboo *(Nandina domestica)*. Evergreen. A light, airy shrub with an oriental, bamboo-like feel, it has many slender, unbranched stems bearing softly textured leaves divided into leaflets. Pinkish-bronze foliage gradually turns green, then picks up a purple or bronze tinge in fall, and becomes scarlet in the winter sun. Although it grows 6 to 8 feet, it is easily controlled. It produces bright red berries in fall on the female plants if one male plant is nearby. The plant is hardy to 5°F.

Hinoki False Cypress *(Chamaecyparis obtusa)*. Evergreen. Slow to outgrow its place and easy to keep below 6 feet, this tree can be trained to reveal its attractive, irregular branching pattern. The Dwarf Hinoki Cypress (*C. obtusa* 'Nana'), growing only 3 feet high, is round-headed with deep green foliage on layered branches. The Golden Hinoki Cypress (*C. obtusa* 'Aurea') has golden new foliage that gradually turns deep green. All Hinoki False Cypress make excellent bonsai specimens. They are unsatisfactory in hot-summer areas, and are hardy to 10°F.

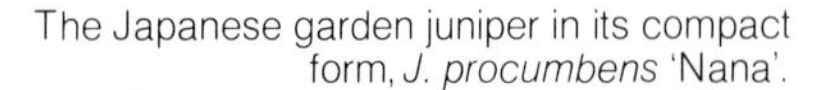

The Japanese garden juniper in its compact form, *J. procumbens* 'Nana'.

Holly *(Ilex* species*)*. Evergreen. The glossy green foliage and bright red berries are a classic reminder of the holiday season. For large, long-lasting berries on a slow-growing compact plant, try Chinese holly *(Ilex cornuta* 'Burfordii Nana'*)*. It is hardy to 0°F. The many forms of English holly (*I. aquifolium*) are just as good in containers, though less tolerant of dry heat. These are hardy to 0°F.

Hydrangea *(H. macrophylla)*. Deciduous. This shrub creates a soft feeling that seems to invite relaxation. Large clusters of white, pink, red, or blue flowers hide the foliage in summer and fall. Flower color is easily manipulated by soil pH, turning blue in acid soil and deepest red in alkaline. Large leaves (8 inches) are glossy and toothed. It has an even, round habit. Prune to desired size. Grow it in full sun in cool-summer areas, in afternoon shade in hot-summer areas. It is hardy to -10°F.

Japanese Black Pine *(Pinus thunbergiana)*. Evergreen. A favorite for bonsai training, it is equally valuable as a tub specimen. Slow growing, it may take three to four years to reach 4 feet. It responds well to pruning, and is hardy in all areas.

Juniper. Evergreen. These handsome patio companions come in enough forms to fit any garden need. The slow growth of *Juniperus chinensis* 'San Jose' makes it a top container shrub. Semi-prostrate and very compact, it has sage-green foliage. It does well trained into formal shapes, or as a bonsai specimen. The Hollywood juniper *(J. chinensis* 'Torulosa') is an erect shrub (10 feet) with artistically twisted branches that are easy to train. The Blue Pfitzer *(J. chinensis* 'Pfitzerana Glauca') has silver-blue foliage on arching stems (10 feet), and can be trained into many shapes. It is hardy in all areas. (For lower growing junipers suitable for hanging baskets, see pages 48-49).

Korean Boxwood *(Buxus microphylla* variety *koreana).* Deciduous. Although well-known as a small hedge or edging plant, this boxwood is most picturesque when trained into formal shapes and planted in containers. It stays low growing (3 feet) and compact without severe pruning, and has pleasant, bright green leaves. It grows well in sun or partial shade. It is hardy to -15°F.

Mugho Pine *(Pinus mugo).* Evergreen. This pine is an ideal candidate for containers. Keep it small by pinching out new, soft green shoots (candles) to 1 inch in spring. Foliage is deep and pleasantly full, and the plant is hardy in all areas.

Natal Plum *(Carissa grandiflora).* Evergreen. This is one of the few shrubs that puts on a year-round show. Large, star-shaped, white flowers borne throughout the year have a wonderful, jasmine-like fragrance. Bright red, edible, 1- to 2-inch fruits taste somewhat like sweet cranberries; use them in sauces, jams, and pies. Leaves are leathery and slightly glossy. Thorned branches are easy to train into formal shapes. 'Boxwood Beauty' and 'Tomilson' are extremely compact, thornless varieties. It is hardy to 25°F.

Oregon Grape *(Mahonia aquifolium).* Evergreen. Good for year-round color. Leaves are divided into many spiny leaflets resembling holly leaves. Bronzy-red new growth gradually turns dark green, then gets purplish or bronze in winter cold and full sun. Yellow flower clusters in spring are followed by long-lasting, dark purple fruits. Control shape and size by pruning. The plant is hardy to -20°F., with protection.

A juniper which might have been overlooked in a nursery can (top) was replanted in a small container and took on a "bonsai" look.

The Japanese black pine *(Pinus thunbergiana)*, shown in the right of the photo, is one of the favorite bonsai pines.

This mugho pine is transformed by transplanting it from a box to a bowl.

Potentilla *(Potentilla fruticosa).* Deciduous. A carefree container plant, this shrub withstands heat, drought, poor soil, and cold temperatures. Yellow to orange flowers bloom from late spring to early fall. Grayish-green to green foliage has divided leaflets. It grows low (1 to 4 feet), with a mounding habit. 'Klondike' is one cultivar that stands out as a prolific bloomer with a compact habit. It is hardy in all areas.

Purple Leaf Japanese Barberry *(Berberis thunbergii* 'Atropurpurea'*).* Deciduous. The finely textured, colorful foliage of this shrub makes it a good portable barrier. Leaves are bronzy-red in spring and summer, and yellow, orange, and red in fall. Red berries are revealed after the leaves drop. It has a dense habit and arching, heavily thorned branches. It can be sheared, but it's more attractive when pruned selectively. Grow it in full sun. It is hardy to -20°F.

Silverberry *(Elaegnus pungens).* Evergreen. The gray-green foliage of this shrub adds a silvery sparkle wherever it's used. Brownish flecks on leaves and stem reflect the sunlight. On its own, it grows as a low, sprawling shrub, but it is easy to keep neat by pruning. It is a tough container plant, good for wind and sun protection. It is available in variegated leaf forms and is hardy to 15°F.

Spiraea *(Spiraea* species*).* Deciduous. The long bloom and dwarf, compact habit (2 to 3 feet) of *Spiraea bumalda* 'Anthony Waterer' justify its use on the patio. It bears flat-topped clusters of rosy-pink flowers from late spring to fall. The fountain-shaped *S. vanhouttei* also deserves attention; its blue-green leaves grow on gracefully arching branches, and it sports showy white flowers. Because flowers are borne on new growth, the plants benefit from heavy pruning. When to prune depends on the variety—summer for spring bloomers, late winter or early spring for summer-flowering varieties. It is hardy to -20°F.

Trees for Containers

If you find your favorite tree missing, it may be because this list includes only those trees that particularly deserve the extra pruning and shaping necessary for container display.

Amur Maple *(Acer ginnala).* Deciduous. This ranks as one of the most brilliant fall-colored maples. Whether it is trained as a single- or multiple-trunked tree, its bright scarlet leaves will brighten up your patio in autumn. Don't keep the Amur maple hidden until fall, though; its small, fragrant spring flowers are followed by red-winged fruits highlighting the beautiful, dense green foliage. It is hardy in all areas.

Bottlebrush *(Callistemon* species*)*. Evergreen. Bottlebrush makes a good summer companion for any patio. Its bright red flowers resemble stiff bottle scrubbers. It blooms from late spring to summer, but it may flower occasionally throughout the year. In containers, try the Lemon Bottlebrush *(C. citrinus)*, and the Weeping Bottlebrush *(C. viminalis)*. These subtropical trees will tolerate only a light frost.

Lemon Bottlebrush. Erect. Hardy. Profuse bloom. Leaves are 3 inches long. Young foliage has a coppery tinge.

Weeping Bottlebrush. Drooping branches. Leaves are 6 inches long. May need support and pruning. 'McCaskilli' is a better-behaved cultivar.

Carolina Cherry Laurel *(Prunus caroliniana)*. Evergreen. No bright, unusual colors here—this is just a dense, glossy tree that offers a luxurious touch of green. Small white flowers bloom in late winter or early spring, with black berries following. Whether single- or multiple-trunked, it is easily trained into formal shapes. Two cultivars ideal for containers are 'Bright-n-Tight' and 'Compacta'. The plant will take cold down to 0°F.

A crape myrtle tree, photographed at the nursery in late August.

Crape Myrtle *(Lagerstroemia indica)*. Deciduous. In summer, when flowering trees are hard to find, the crape myrtle comes across in style. Crinkled, crepe-like flowers in shades of white, pink, rose, or lavender bloom over a long period. The light green leaves turn orangish-red in fall. The mottled tan bark and branching pattern are more apparent during the leafless winter months and add a note of interest to a possibly bland landscape. The root system is sufficiently cold-hardy to encourage cold-winter use. A group of crape myrtles called Indian Tribe have superior hardiness, performance, and mildew resistance. Named cultivars are: red-flowering 'Cherokee', purple-flowering 'Catawba', pink-flowering 'Potomac' and 'Seminole', and light lavender 'Powhatan'. The tree is generally hardy to 0°F., but check the tolerance of individual cultivars.

Eastern Redbud *(Cercis canadensis)*. Deciduous. For an early spring flower show, the redbud will satisfy even the most demanding observer. Small, pea-like clusters of pink, purple, or white flowers completely cover the leafless branches. Heart-shaped leaves provide summer shade ideal for patios, and turn yellow in fall. Showy seed pods are revealed in late fall after the leaves drop; they remain on the tree into winter. Of the many cultivars, 'Forest Pansy' is of interest, with pinkish-purple flowers and foliage on red stems. 'Alba' is a profuse-flowering variety. The tree is hardy in all areas except for those with winter temperatures below -20°F.

Evergreen Pear *(Pyrus kawakamii)*. Evergreen. Left untouced, it becomes a sprawling shrub. Tied to a trellis or wire, it easily can be trained as an espalier. Staked, it makes a handsome single-trunked tree. The glossy green foliage is a year-round attraction. Fragrant white flowers are abundant in late winter or early spring. It is fast growing. Heavy pruning reduces flowering. It may not survive extreme cold.

Flowering Crabapple *(Malus* species*)*. Considering the many varieties of crabapple available, there's surely one to fit your garden scheme. Widely admired for the delicate, profuse spring flowers in shades of white, pink, and red, the crabapples come in a wide range of habits and foliage colors as well. The tree shape ranges from weeping to columnar. Leaf color is primarily green, but some leaves retain a reddish-bronze color for the entire season. Fruits are attractive from fall to early winter. When selecting a variety of crabapple, be sure to watch for disease resistance and hardiness of individual cultivars. These crabapples suitable for containers have acceptable disease resistance:

Japanese Flowering Crabapple *(M. floribunda)*. Horizontally branching. Mound-like. Flowers are pink, fading to white. Fruits are yellow-red (3/8 inch).

Parkman Crabapple (*M. halliana* 'Parkmanii'). Gracefully arching purple branches. Flowers are large, double, rose. Fruits are dull red (¼ inch).

Cultivar 'Red Silver'. Irregularly branched, yet graceful. Reddish or purplish-bronze foliage. Flowers are deep wine red. Fruits are purplish (¾ inch).

Sargent Crabapple (*M. sargentii*). Lowest and broadest of the crabapples (8-10 feet high × 12 feet wide). Flowers are white. Fruits are small, red, in clusters.

Flowering Dogwood (*Cornus florida*). Deciduous. The flowering dogwood signals the beginning of spring with a spectacular show, and it deserves to be featured in your landscape. Flowers appear before foliage, in shades of red, pink, rose, or white. Foliage turns bright red in fall, highlighted by red berries. Its slow growth when young (to 10 to 15 feet) makes it a good container candidate. It also is a perfect companion for the eastern redbud. It is hardy to -20°F.

Flowering Plums (*Prunus* species). When you think about the flowering plums, you have to consider more than the spring flowers alone; their purple foliage is a strong element in any garden.

Prunus cerasifera 'Atropurpurea' and its related forms—'Thundercloud', 'Newportii', 'Vesuvius'—are widely available.

P.× blireiana is the popular fruitless tree. It has reddish-bronze foliage and bears pink double flowers, in contrast to the pink single clusters of the 'Atropurpurea' forms. *P. blireiana* also has a lighter, more graceful form than the 'Atropurpurea' and its variations. It is hardy in all areas.

Ginkgo (*Ginkgo biloba*). Deciduous. This large tree can be held to container size for years. Its light green, fan-shaped leaves dance in the wind, but always provide a summer-long attraction whether moving or still. In the fall, the leaves turn a rich, bright yellow. The fact that this prehistoric species survivor is sometimes called the oldest tree on earth hints at its hardiness and versatility. Give it the toughest spot in the garden and watch it thrive. To be sure you get a male tree (fruits of the females are messy and have an unpleasant smell), choose named cultivars such as 'Autumn Gold', 'Lakeview', or 'Sentry'. Ginkgo is hardy to -20°F.

Variegated *Pieris*, dwarfed by long life in a nursery can, is reborn and raised high with the ground cover blue star creeper.

Glossy Privet (*Ligustrum lucidum*). Evergreen. An admirable performer in large tubs, the glossy privet will reach tree size quickly and thrive in tight quarters for years. Large feathery clusters of white flowers appear in spring, followed by dark blue fruits in quantity. The foliage is luxuriant, almost deep green, and glossy. Easily trained into many shapes, single- or multiple-trunked, it is hardy to 20°F.

Golden Rain Tree (*Koelreuteria paniculata*). Deciduous. Uncommon summer color abounds from this well-behaved tree. Large clusters of yellow flowers appear in midsummer. New foliage is salmon-colored in spring. Long leaves (12 to 15 inches) are divided into leaflets. Fruits are papery, resembling Japanese lanterns, and last into winter. Fairly slow growth (10 to 15 feet) makes it a good container tree. It is hardy to -20°F.

Holly (*Ilex* species). Some hollies have no spines on the leaves; some don't look like "hollies"; some have black fruits and others red fruits; some are low-spreading dwarfs; and some are small trees. Here are a few of the most useful:

The Japanese holly (*Ilex crenata*) bears no resemblance to the Christmas holly. Many resemble boxwood more than they do the conventional holly, and the berries are black. With its small leaves and dark green color, it takes to shearing well. Although it will grow to 8 feet or more, it can be held to any height.

The Chinese holly (*I. cornuta*) and its horticultural form, Burford Chinese holly, are at home in every mild-winter climate. The Burford holly has the elegance of an "entrance" shrub and the toughness of a weed in its ability to grow. Its leaves have almost no spines, and it makes a compact, shiny green shrub 6 to 9 feet high. The berries are bright red. These two species are hardy to 0° F.

Yaupon holly *(I. vomitoria)* is a native of the South. It grows as a large shrub or small tree up to 20 feet high. Its red fruits are quite showy. Dwarf forms are available. It is hardy only to about 10° F.

Japanese Maple *(Acer palmatum).* The Japanese maple in its various forms is commonly used in cool-summer Northwest gardens, and as a dainty, small, containerized tree it can be held in a tub for years, since it grows slowly. Many grafted garden forms are smaller than the seedlings. Of these, you might consider:

'Burgundy Lace'. Soft lacy effect. Deeply cut, serrated burgundy leaves on green stems.

'Dissectum'. Easily trained. Low, weeping habit. Finely cut, fern-like green leaves are scarlet in fall.

Most cultivars are hardy to -20°F.

The Japanese maple is slow-growing and can be kept in a container for years.

Loquat *(Eriobotrya japonica).* Evergreen. For a close-up, tropical effect, this tree certainly deserves attention. Large (12-inch) leaves are heavily veined, deeply toothed, dark green on top, and fuzzy, brownish-red beneath. It is less than showy, but the extremely fragrant white flowers will fill your garden with a spicy scent in fall. It bears attractive yellow, edible fruits in winter. Selective pruning will hold it to container size (10 to 12 feet) for years. Cut branches are good for arrangements. This subtropical fruit tree is hardy to 0°F. but will only bear fruit in warmer climates.

Naked Coral Tree *(Erythrina coralloides).* Deciduous. This tree is an eye-catcher every season: in spring, it produces fiery-red, pinecone-like blossoms; in summer, its large leaves provide shade; in late autumn, the leaves turn yellow and drop; and in winter, the tree's interesting shape and branching patterns never go unnoticed. This tender tree won't tolerate any frost.

Oleander *(Nerium oleander).* Evergreen. If trained as a single-trunked tree and placed in a container, this normally dense, sprawling shrub will add color to the patio when tree color is hard to come by. It blooms generously from late spring to early fall, accented handsomely by somewhat leathery, dark green foliage. Choose from a wide range of colors—pink, rose, red, salmon, light yellow, and white. The foliage is damaged at 10°F. but recovers in spring. This is not a good plant to have around children, however, as all parts of it are very poisonous.

Palms. Evergreen. Several palms make very fine container trees. The Parlor Palm *(Chamaedorea elegans)* has typical fish-skeleton-like leaves which sheath the single trunk, emerging in a cluster at the top.

The Paradise Palm *(Howea forsteriana)* has similar leaves on a clean, interestingly scarred, 9-foot stem.

The Pygmy Date Palm *(Phoenix roebelenii)* grows slowly to 6 feet. Its airy leaves emerge from the top of the slender stem.

The Lady Palm (*Rhapis excelsa*), an old favorite in containers, grows 6 to 12 feet tall. Its many stalks bear oriental-fan-like foliage at the tips, making for a bushy, bamboo-like effect.

Strictly tropical plants, palms won't take freezing.

Pineapple Guava *(Feijoa sellowiana).* Evergreen. Normally, the pineapple guava grows as a dense, gray-green shrub noteworthy for its flowers and fruit, but it's at its best when pruned and trained as a picturesque small tree. Flowers are made up of four thick white petals, tinged purplish beneath, and a big tuft of bright red stamens. The fleshy petals are edible, as are the soft fruits, 2 to 4 inches long, which are filled with juicy, aromatic pulp. Unusually hardy for a subtropical, it will take a 15°F. frost.

Containers of dwarf oleanders with marigolds.

Above: The fernlike, almost feathery leaves of the silk tree give it a soft, gentle feeling.

Right: Container-grown wisteria trained as a large shrub.

Silk Tree *(Albizia julibrissin)*. Deciduous. A soft, gentle feeling seems to prevail around this tree. Light green, fern-like leaves seem infinitely divided, almost feathery. Being light-sensitive, they fold at night. Branches arch to form a flat-topped canopy that provides excellent filtered shade. Pink flower puffs are held above the foliage in summer. Although it grows quickly, it nevertheless maintains container size (10 to 15 feet) for years. It will stand 0°F.

Sour Gum *(Nyssa sylvatica)*. Deciduous. The drooping branches of this picturesque tree bear lustrous, dark green leaves that form a very dense head of great ornamental value. In fall, the leaves turn a dazzling scarlet-orange. This tree is certain to be the focal point in any garden. It bears inconspicuous flowers in spring, followed by dark blue fruits in summer (usually hidden by foliage). It is hardy everywhere.

Southern Magnolia *(Magnolia grandiflora)*. Evergreen. Few things are easier to live with than the spring elegance of the magnolia. Large (up to 10 inches across), fragrant flowers bloom in spring to early summer in shades of white, pink, and purple. Interesting, colorful seed capsules follow the flowers. Leaves are giant (up to 12 inches long by 5 inches wide), stiff, and glossy green.

Magnolias outgrow containers eventually, but smaller, slow-growing forms of Southern magnolia, like 'St. Mary', are handsome in boxes for years. Although a southern native, magnolia is usually hardy to 0°F.

Sunburst Honey Locust *(Gleditsia triacanthos* var. *inermis)*. Deciduous. This tree makes up for its lack of flower color with golden-yellow new foliage highlighted by the older, light green leaves. The overall effect is of a wonderful yellow canopy from spring to fall. Softly textured leaves are finely divided into small leaflets. The entire tree turns yellowish-gold in fall. Ideal for close quarters and containers. It is hardy everywhere.

Ternstroemia *(Ternstroemia gymnanthera)*. Evergreen. This is pleasant to be around because of its fragrance and slow-growing enough to keep in a tub for a long time. The leaves begin as a showy bronze-red and gradually turn anywhere from green to purplish-red, depending on temperature and exposure. The deepest reds and purples come from cool temperatures and full sun. Prune to shape. Inconspicuous yet fragrant yellow flowers are followed by yellow berries. It is hardy to 0°F.

Washington Thorn *(Crataegus phaenopyrum).* Put this tree in a container on your patio and you'll be rewarded with color through spring, summer, and fall. White flowers bloom profusely in spring to early summer. Attractive clusters of red berries appear in late summer through winter. Lobed leaves are brilliant orange-red in fall. It has a dense, graceful, low-branching habit. It is hardy to -20°F.

Wisteria *(Wisteria* species*).* Deciduous. This vigorous vine can be trained as a small, single-trunked tree with an umbrella-like top. The "tree" produces the same long, lovely clusters of blossoms that make this woody plant the "queen of the vines." Fragrant flowers are borne in spring in shades of white, pink, or lavender. Leaves (12 to 18 inches long) are divided into leaflets. Wisteria is good in containers and is hardy to -20°F.

Yew Pine *(Podocarpus macrophyllus).* This slow-growing tree is valuable indoors and out. Leaves are long (4 inches) and narrow. The yellowish-green new foliage contrasts nicely with the older, dark green leaves, giving a fern-like effect. Good in containers. A tender native of Japan, it will tolerate temperatures down to 10°F.

Left: Many strong-growing Southern Indian azaleas can be trained as standards.
Right: This dwarf Alberta spruce has been left in its original nursery can since 1958.

For most people, daffodils announce the arrival of spring.

GROWING BULBS IN CONTAINERS

These flowers mean spring to many people in colder climates, and forcing bulbs indoors can brighten cold winter days.

No group of flowers offers a brighter array of color than bulbs; and no spring would be complete without a generous splash of their vivid hues.

Because the container garden can allow great versatility, you can provide a display of flowers starting during the bleak winters months and continuing through spring. Schedule some bulbs for early bloom by using the florist's method of *forcing;* have a follow-up list for other blooms that will flower naturally in early spring.

Forcing bulbs in containers is easy, but you have to plan ahead and think about spring when it's only autumn. Wintertime is too late to start forcing spring bulbs to bloom three or four months ahead of schedule. You may as well have planted them and let them bloom naturally.

Your choice of bulbs and containers has a lot to do with your success (see bulb chart, page 78). You can ask for planning assistance at your local nursery or you can consult bulb catalogs. Bulbs often are divided into spring and fall types. This refers to when they should be planted, not to when they bloom. If you're ordering through a catalog, give yourself enough time; choose types and colors no later than early summer.

After your container-grown bulbs have bloomed (forced or not), don't save them to be grown in the same way again next season. Instead, put them out in the ground to regain the vigor to develop flowers in future years. Start with new bulbs for your containers next season.

Spring is the time to choose your bulbs—not only to get a jump on the season but also to get the best selection. If you're not familiar with names and their colors or with the new introductions, ask your nurseryman for help. The size of the bulb dictates the size container to use. Flower colors usually are indicated clearly in the display for each kind and variety.

Plan to use only a *single* variety in each container; even in the same species, one color may bloom before another, and in the spotlight of a single container the resulting display may be patchy and unattractive. Don't be stingy with bulbs—think in terms of masses of color. If you want many colors, grow several containers, each with only *one* variety, for the most pleasing effects.

By shifting containers that bear blooms of different colors, you can achieve a veritable kaleidoscope of spring. As each container's show of color disappears, you can remove it from center stage and replace it with the next colorful performer. If you stagger the plantings, you can extend your flowering spring. For instance, try potting three containers at a time and placing them in storage at two-week intervals. Your spring show should come off on schedule: each group will enter the stage as its predecessor exits.

To grow hyacinths, plant one to a single 4-inch pot instead of putting the bulbs directly into a large container. This extra step lets you see just what you're dealing with: by blooming time, hyacinths vary considerably in height, color, and time of bloom. When they flower, transfer them to display pots.

Some tiny jewels *(Iris danfordiae)* of the bulb world are brought into focus when placed in containers. The traditional use for these bulbs is in rock gardens.

Don't Overlook Miniatures

There's no need to restrict miniature flowering bulbs to rock gardens; they also are delightful in pots.

To keep the dainty *Iris danfordiae* (see photo) from getting lost in a border or bed, bring it closer to the eye (this works well for many miniatures). Check the bulb catalogs for the miniatures of crocus, iris, daffodils, and other bulbs. Whenever rock garden bulbs are discussed, visualize the flowers in a pot or bowl display.

It's easy to transfer bulbs from a rock garden to a container garden. Here's how Reginald Farrer describes rock garden crocus in his classic work, *The English Rock Garden*:

"*Crocus imperati* is one of the very loveliest, emitting, first, its prostrate dark leaves, and then, wrapped in twin spathes, a chalice of blossom, opaque creamy buff outside, and feathered richly with lines of dark purple . . . .

"*Crocus ancyrensis* (Golden Bunch) opens in February, a little golden star rarely touched with brown, and with scarlet stigmata.

"*Crocus susianus* (Cloth of Gold, [now called *C. angustifolius*]) has cups of brilliant orange gold, heavily striped with dark brown varnish outside, and

Bulbs for Containers

Name	Height	Planting Depth	Exposure* S	PS	FS	Planting Season	Flowering Season	Comment
Allium (Flowering Onion)	9-60″	2-4″ depends on size	•			Fall	Depends on species; spring-summer	Many species in a wide range of colors. Long bloom season. Small species like *A. neapolitanum* are ideal for containers.
Agapanthus	18-48″	Just below surface	•	•		Spring or fall	Midsummer	Leave in same container year after year. Divide only infrequently—every 5-6 years. Evergreen dwarf forms 'Dwarf White' and 'Peter Pan' (blue) are fine when potted.
Anemone	6-24″	1-2″	•	•		See text	Late winter-early spring	See text. Red, pink, blue, rose, or white flowers.
Begonia, tuberous	12-20″	Just covered ½″		•	•	Winter	Summer-fall	Flowers in many shades of red, pink, yellow, orange, or white. Becomes leggy in dense shade. Best in filtered shade, cool temperature, high humidity.
Caladium	9-30″	Just covered		•	•	Spring	————	See text. Red, pink, green, and white foliage colors. With proper storage, it can be left in the same container.
Canna, dwarf	18-30″	5-6″	•			Midspring	Late summer-early fall	Large flowers in many colors. Attractive, tropical-looking green or bronze foliage. With proper frost-free storage, it can be left in same container. Remove faded flowers after bloom. After blooming cut stalk at soil level.
Clivia	12-36″	Top just above soil		•	•	Fall	Early spring	Yellow, orange, or red flowers. Use as indoor plant in cold-climate areas. If kept moist, it can be left in the same container.
Crinum	24-36″	Neck exposed		•		Spring or fall	Spring-summer	Flowers in shades of white or pink, often striped red. Best left undisturbed in container moved into frost-free place.
Crocus	4-5″	Just covered	•	•		Fall	Depends on species; generally, late winter-early spring	See text for variety description. Flowers in shades of blue, purple, gold, and white. In warm areas, refrigerate 4 weeks prior to planting. Withhold water in summer.
Dahlia	12-48″	6″ (fill gradually)	•	•		Spring or fall	Summer	Many flower forms and colors; dwarf varieties best for containers.
Freesia	10-18″	2″ deep	•			Fall	Late winter-early spring	Flowers white, pink, red, lavender, purple, blue, yellow, and orange. Fragrant. May need staking, Tender in cold climates. Grow indoors until frost is past.

opening into a wide star with so much heartiness that the segments often go too far and turn down the other way. It opens with the first warmth of the February sun and is a native of southern Russia.

"*Crocus chrysanthus* can be told from all other golden crocus by the black spot on the barb of the anthers. The species is most variable but invariably beautiful, the type being of pure stainless yellow, but the forms diverge on to sulphur-yellow and differing shades of blue, with diversities of blue feathering."

At certain times of the day, the alabaster white of these hybrid tulips, planted in a clay chicken-shaped container, catches the sparkle of natural back lighting.

Selecting the Containers

Your selection of containers will be limited only by the number of bulbs, the depth of the pot (always allow at least 2 inches of potting soil beneath the bulb for good root development), and the need for a drainage hole.

Your containers can be formal, as casual as a coconut shell, as classic as a clay pot, or as whimsical as a pot in the shape of a fish or chicken (see photos). Bonsai containers lend themselves especially well to bulb display. Bulbs such as *Narcissus minimus*, the tiniest of the trumpet daffodils, are striking in a glazed bonsai container.

Once you've selected your containers and bulbs, you're ready to plant. The following pages outline the procedures.

Bulbs for Containers

Name	Height	Planting Depth	Exposure* S	PS	FS	Planting Season	Flowering Season	Comment
Hippeastrum (Amaryllis)	24-36"	Half covered	•	•		Available late October	Indoors, begins 4-6 weeks after planting	Best indoors or frostproof outdoor area. Flowers large, in shades of red, pink, and white.
Hyacinthus (Hyacinth)	6-12"	5"	•			Fall	Early spring	Refrigerate bulbs for 6 weeks in warm-winter areas. Many soft pastel shades. Dutch types are fragrant. Bulb size relates directly to size of flower spike.
Iris, Dutch	10-24"	Covered 1"	•	•		Midfall	Early spring in mild areas—late spring in cold	Flowers in blue, purple, yellow, orange, and white shades. Plant 5 to a 6" pot. Good for forcing.
Ixia	18-24"	Covered 2"	•			Fall	Late spring	Flowers in red, pink, yellow, orange, and white with dark centers. Tender. See Freesia.
Lilium (Lily)	18-60"	5-6" (fill gradually)	•	•		Late fall or early spring	Spring-summer (depends on variety)	Many flower forms and colors. Plant bulbs as soon as you get them. Require constant moisture but excellent drainage. One bulb to a 6" pot; several to larger container.
Narcissus (Daffodil)	5-20"	Covered 2½ times width of bulb	•	•		Early fall	Spring	Plant early and late varieties for extended blooming season. Many single and bicolor shades of red, orange, yellow and white 'Angel Tears' and 'Hoop Petticoat' are perfect dwarf varieties for small containers.
Ornithogalum (Star of Bethlehem)	10-14"	4-5"	•	•		Early fall	Midspring	White flowers with contrasting green stripe on each petal (*O. Umbellatum*).
Ranunculus	10-24"	Covered 1"	•			Winter	Late spring-early summer	See text; flowers in shades of red, pink, yellow, orange, and white; best in cool climates.
Tigridia	18-30"	2-4"	•	•		Early spring	Mid to late summer	Large flowers in red, pink, yellow, and white shades with dark speckles.
Tulipa (Tulip)	5-30"	2½ times width of bulb —4" to 6"	•	•		October. Late as December in frost-free areas	Spring—depends on variety	Many flower colors and varieties; don't ignore species tulips like *Tulipa kaulmanniana* ('The Water-lily tulip')—they are ideal in pots. Require 4-5-week cold period. In warm-winter areas, refrigerate 4 weeks prior to planting.

*S = sun; PS = part shade; FS = full shade

How To Plant Bulbs in Containers

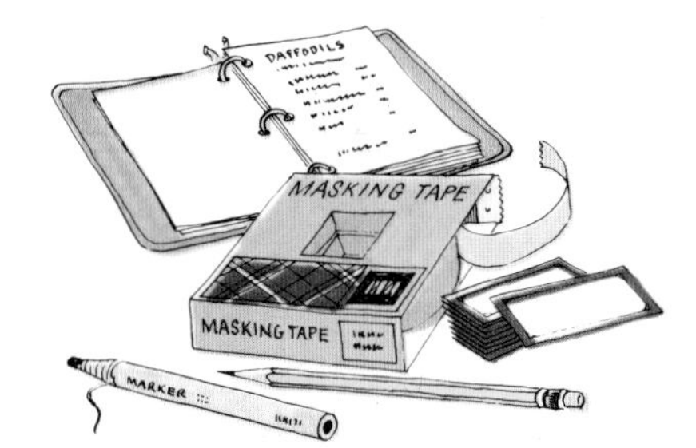

Some materials needed.

Check and enlarge drainage hole if necessary.

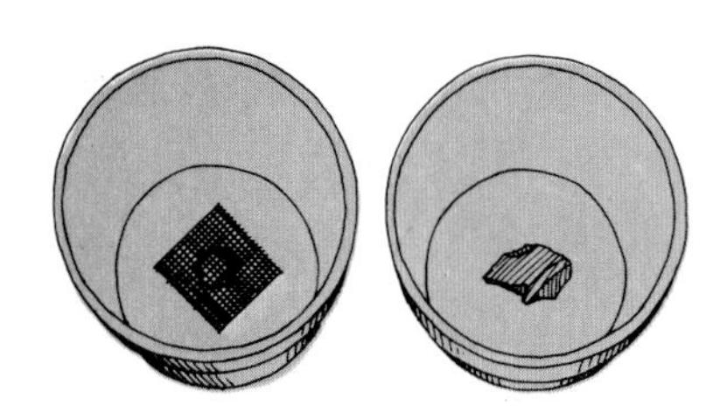
Cover drainage hole.

Fill the container with planter mix.

Plant the bulbs.

Bulbs covered with shredded polystyrene

Before you leave the nursery, make sure that each bulb variety is labeled properly. As for soil, a packaged planter mix is sterile and easy to use. Plan to use a light planter mix that won't become compacted. Keep permeability and drainage in mind (see pages 25-27).

Referring to the bulb chart (page 78), make a tag for each pot. Then take out the bulbs (one group at a time) and place them shoulder to shoulder in the empty pot, allowing only a ¼ to ½ inch separation for soil. Follow this procedure with each group of bulbs, being certain not to get them mixed up. Check the bulb chart for the length of time to anticipate before bloom, and the normal flowering period (late spring, midspring, etc.). This is the time to schedule your spring-in-winter succession of flowers. Use a waterproof pencil or pen to mark a strip of masking tape with the date to be planted and stored, and the approximate date to expect blooming. You can remove this tape easily at flowering time. Put the name tags and bulbs in containers, labeled. It is important to remove the bulbs from the bag they come in and store them in dry, cool conditions.

Keep simple records in a small notebook kept in your work area. Record the necessary data for each container: "name of bulb"; "date entered cold storage"; then, later, "date removed from cold storage."

Write down any additional information you can think of—it might be helpful the following year. (It is surprising how much detail you forget from one planting season to the next.) These records will help you establish a good blooming schedule in succeeding years and point up any flaws in your original planning. You'll want to repeat your successes and correct any mistakes.

After this "dry-run" planning, you're ready to proceed. *Make sure to concentrate on one container at a time.*

Step 1. Check the container to be sure the drainage hole is adequate. If using a clay or plastic pot, enlarge the hole with a drill. (A hand rasp or "Stickleback" drill is handy for this job.)

Step 2. Cover the drainage hole with window screen or curved pieces from a broken pot. This allows the water to drain, but not the planter mix.

Step 3. Add a bottom layer of planter mix deep enough so that the tops of the bulbs will be 1 inch below the container rim.

Step 4. Plant the flat end (not the pointed end) facing down. If you plant the bulb upside down, it will right itself; but it will take longer, throwing off your show schedule and wasting the bulb's energy needlessly.

Step 5. Place the bulbs shoulder to shoulder in the pot, firming them in gently so that they nest into the potting soil (points up). The bulbs are in the top of the container to allow room for root growth.

Step 6. Once the bulbs are in place, add more planter mix to cover them.

Step 7. Water thoroughly by setting the container in a pail of water and letting it soak until the surface of the soil feels moist. Allow the excess to drain from the bottom of the container. It is now ready for "cold storage." Repeat this for all containers that you want to go into cold treatment right away.

Step 8. Plant the bulbs intended for staggered planting in subsequent weeks the same as described above, but leave them *dry*. Be sure to mark your calendar—when their time comes, water as above and put them into the cold treatment phase on schedule.

Step 9. Place containers where they can get 12 to 14 weeks of cold treatment—temperatures between 40° and 50°. Any spot that's cold and dark is satisfactory. An unheated cellar or vegetable storage unit is ideal.

How to store your containers depends on your climate. In moderately cold winters, it's all right to store them outdoors by covering them with peat moss or similar material in a trench or box. Shredded polystyrene is an excellent mulch. It is lightweight, never freezes, and allows water to pass through readily. In severe winter climates, store containers where they won't freeze.

Where winters are too warm to provide a sufficient cold period of 12 to 14 weeks, refrigerate hardy bulbs (especially tulips) for 6 weeks before planting in containers.

The purpose of chilling the bulbs in storage is to give them the environment they need to develop a strong root system to support future shoot and flower production.

During this storage period, roots require moisture for growth. Not only must the soil be moist when the containers are placed in storage, but they must be kept *moist* (not wet) throughout the storage treatment.

So far, the procedure for growing bulbs for display in containers *outdoors* is the same as for "forcing" bulbs for early bloom *indoors*.

At this point, however, the procedures differ. For indoor display, "force" early bloom by gradually giving the bulbs higher temperatures and light. For outdoor display, do nothing. Let the flowering come naturally.

Step 10. Now the forcing. At the end of the 12 to 14 cold weeks, when the sprouts are 2 to 5 inches high and the roots can be seen at the drainage hole, place the containers in a cool 60°F. room. After a week or two, they are ready to receive normal room temperature. Be sure to give them adequate light at this point or the growth will be leggy.

After bloom, keep the leaves growing as long as you can. If you plan to put the bulbs out in the garden when true spring arrives, put them in a cool place (50°-55°F.). Never remove the leaves until they are brown and papery. Food manufactured in the leaves is stored in the bulb for next season's growth. For more information on forcing bulbs, see the next section on How To Force Hardy Bulbs.

Plants staggered for planting in subsequent weeks.

One rewarding aspect of indoor gardening is persuading plants to bloom out of season. By duplicating (but shortening) the stages bulbs go through in your garden, you can have tulips, daffodils, and hyacinths blooming indoors while the snow piles up outdoors. And if your winter climate is warmer, you can enjoy these spring bulbs ahead of time, too.

In addition to bulbs, there are also some hardy perennials that respond to this treatment—hosta, astilbe, bleeding-heart, and lily-of-the-valley.

You can also plant annual flowers for a sunny indoor garden, as well as forcing cut branches of favorite flowering shrubs.

A display of spring-flowering bulbs about an entryway.

How To Force Hardy Bulbs

It's easy to force tulips, daffodils, ornithogalum, hyacinths, and the little bulbs —crocuses, snowdrops, and grape-hyacinths—to bloom indoors ahead of their normal outdoor time. Grow them as Christmas gifts for friends. Read the catalogs carefully, and select the largest bulbs obtainable. It doesn't pay to buy anything but the best when you use bulbs for forcing. Choose those the firm recommends for forcing, or buy the ones listed on page 83. If you order by September, the bulbs will be delivered in early fall. Then follow these instructions:

Soil mixture. The soil mixture for bulbs can be made up of equal parts soil, sand, and peat moss. To each 5-inch pot of this mix, add a teaspoon of bone meal. If you don't want to bother mixing soil, buy a soilless medium. However, this is costly for large quantities. (For how to mix your own soilless medium, see page 25).

Pot size. The kind and quantity of bulbs you plan to plant determine what size container to use. One large daffodil or tulip bulb can be planted in a 4- or 5-inch diameter pot in which three crocuses or other smaller bulbs would fit. For six tulips, daffodils, or hyacinths, you'll need a 6- to 10-inch pot. When you plant these large bulbs, cover the tops of tulips and hyacinths with ½ inch of soil. With daffodils, don't try to cover their necks—just the fattened portion of the bulb. Cover smaller bulbs like crocuses with ½ inch of soil. Then water thoroughly. You also can purchase pre-planted containers of bulbs that are conditioned to begin the forcing process.

Temperature. Bulbs need a cool period after potting so that they can form a vigorous root system. Without a potful of roots, they cannot bloom prolifically later on. Years ago, the usual practice was to bury these pots of bulbs in a bed of cinders outdoors in a coldframe, leaving them there until at least New Year's Day (except for some pre-conditioned bulbs, which will bloom for Christmas). This system is impractical for most of us today, however; besides, there are easier ways to accomplish the same thing. Find a cool, frost-free place where bulbs can be forced. An unheated garage attached to the house, a cool attic, a cool basement, or a window in the cold room of your basement will do. A temperature range of 35° to 55°F. will promote good root growth. Keep the soil evenly moist throughout this period.

When to start forcing bulbs. You can begin when leaves begin to push upward—usually sometime after January 1. Bring the pots indoors, a few each week so you will have blooms over a longer period, to a sunny, cool (55° to 70°F.) place; keep the soil moist at all times. The cooler the air, the longer the flowers will last. Keep bulbs away from sources of heat such as radiators and gas heaters. Bring all pots to be forced into warmth and light by late February.

Problems in forcing bulbs. Don't expect many, but there are a few. Tulips almost always show some aphids, either on the leaves when they emerge from the soil, or on the flower buds. Spray them carefully with a houseplant insecticide. Flower buds of forced bulbs will blast (fail to open) if the soil is allowed to dry out severely after they've begun to grow. Sometimes bulbs have basal rot (seldom your fault). If foliage suddenly turns yellow and stops growing, give it a gentle tug. Chances are you'll find it loose in the pot, and a rootless, rotted bulb in the soil. Destroy by burning.

After the flowers fade. At this time, keep the foliage in good health by providing moisture and sunlight. As soon as the danger of hard freezing is past outdoors, move the bulbs to an out-of-the-way place where the foliage can continue to mature and store up strength for another year's blooms. Although the bulbs cannot be used for forcing next year, you will find them good additions to the outdoor garden. Plant them when you bring them out of the house, or leave them in the pots until the following autumn, transferring them then to the open ground.

Some large and showy blossoms of tulip 'Gudoshnik' (back) and 'General Eisenhower' (right) form a background for the small *Tulipa batalinii.*

The yellow blossoms of the water lily tulip and daffodil 'Delibes' are good choices for this site with a blue water background.

Narcissus to force. These fragrant-flowered relatives of the daffodil are delightful subjects for forcing in a semi-sunny to sunny location. The bulbs are available in autumn. Plant them in moist pebbles in a bowl, or pot them in a mixture of equal parts soil, sand, and peat moss, kept moist. Either way, place the bases of the bulbs to a depth of 1 to 1½ inches in the growing medium; then water thoroughly. Drain, and set in a cool (50° to 65°F.—no warmer, if possible), dark place for the roots to form. After the bulbs have a good root system (which usually takes two to four weeks), put them in a warm, brightly sunny spot. There they will bloom quickly, in fragrant clusters of white or gold.

After forcing 'Paper-white' or 'Paper-yellow' (cultivars of *Narcissus tazetta*), discard the bulbs if you live where winter cold dips below 20°F. In the South, plant them in the garden outdoors. But don't try to force them again. Buy new stock each year.

Daffodils to force. 'King Alfred' and 'Golden Harvest' are classic, golden, big daffodils that force perfectly. 'President Lebrun' has pale yellow petals and a dark golden cup and forces well. Short-cup varieties good for forcing are 'John Evelyn' and 'Scarlet Leader'. Miniatures, such as 'W. P. Milner', 'March Sunshine', and *Narcissus obvallaris* (Lent-lily), force beautifully and take up little space.

Tulips to force. 'Brilliant Star', 'Ibis', 'Prince of Austria', 'Rising Sun', 'Murillo', 'Scarlet Cardinal', 'Willemsoord', 'Scarlet Admiral', 'Bartigon', 'Niphetos', 'Rose Copland', 'William Pitt', 'Gudoshnik', 'Golden Harvest', and 'Fantasy'.

Hyacinths to force. These include 'Jan Bos', 'L'Innocence', 'Bismarck', 'Gertrude', 'Lady Derby', 'La Victoire', 'Grand Maitre', 'Ostara', 'Perle Brilliante', 'City of Haarlem', 'Queen of Pinks', and 'King of Blues'.

A piece of volcanic rock turns these *Crocus chrysanthus* 'Snow Bunting' into a mini-rockery.

"Little" bulbs to force. Little bulbs such as crocuses, snowdrops, and grape-hyacinths *(Muscari)* sometimes are forced, but their lifespan is so brief indoors that it is really a shame to waste time on them, especially since they last days or even weeks longer when planted naturally outdoors.

Other bulbs to force. In addition to the standbys, consider calla-lily *(Zantedeschia)*, the amaryllis *(Hippeastrum)*, Cape lily (*Veltheimia viridifolia*), freesia, iris *(I. reticulata* and the Dutch, English, and Spanish types), the Easter lily *(Lilium longiflorum)*, shamrock *(Oxalis)*, and Squills *(Scilla siberica)*.

Forcing hyacinths in water. You can grow the hyacinth bulb in water if you place it in specially designed containers or jars, or any type of vase that will hold the bulb in the top and allow the roots to reach into the bottom section. Fill the vase so the base of the bulb just touches the water. A small piece of charcoal in the container will keep the water sweet and retard the development of harmful bacteria. Place it in a dark, cool area until the roots are developed before you move it into the light. Change the water weekly. Flowers and foliage develop rapidly. Use any of the varieties listed previously in this section.

A Special Note About Anemone and Ranunculus Bulbs

You can grow these bulbs successfully in containers, but don't force them. Unlike most other bulbs, they need no special storage temperatures or air circulation—just a rest once their blooming period is over. However, they must be stored dry or they may rot. Under these circumstances, it's not easy to fool them about the seasons. Since they're tender to frost, you can give them an early start indoors by providing good light; just don't keep them cold and moist and dark in storage. Anemone and ranunculus bulbs are worth planting—a spring is not complete without a few tubs of these colorful flowers to brighten any container garden.

These ranunculus were planted in individual pots for easy color arrangement later.

Notes for Mild-Winter Areas

In mild-winter areas, treat yourself to the showy foliage of the caladium. These members of the arum family are tuberous-rooted perennials from tropical America. Classed as "bulbs," they die down in fall and take a bulb-like winter rest. Their "flowers" are interesting but insignificant—caladium is grown purely for its spectacular leaf colors. Store the bulbs dry in vermiculite or peat moss after the foliage dies back. Then, around January, bring them out for potting and reviving for the spring show. They enjoy a night temperature that is constant at not less than 60° F.; keep the potting mix evenly damp. Plant about three tubers to an 8-inch pot, allowing plenty of depth for root development, but don't over-pot. Use any good planter mix. When the first leaves peek through the soil, increase their light from subdued to north window bright. Keep humidity about 60 percent. They'll come along much faster if you use a heating cable beneath the pot. If you don't have one, use this propagating trick.

In mild-climate areas the fancy-leafed caladium, a tuberous-rooted perennial, is an ideal container plant.

7½ watt light bulb
(15 watt max.)
Porcelain socket screwed to blocks
Put the light under an upturned pot with the planted pot on top to keep the soil evenly warm.

As the weather warms outdoors on a shady patio, gradually get the plant used to the outdoor location with other shade plants. The lovely foliage adds color and textural contrast when placed among ferns and *Chamaedorea* palms. Caladiums should have frequent but very light feeding (such as light dilution of fish emulsion) and evenly *dry* soil. Be sure to maintain adequate drainage. Try as many colors as you can locate at your local nursery (or order from specialty growers' catalogs)—they include silver, white, pink, red, bronze, and green in a riotous variety of psychedelic combinations. (Caladiums are also very good house plants if you provide sufficient humidity).

Bulbs and Pests

Pests will usually ignore bulbs planted in containers, but they will take an occasional nibble from the flowering parts. The culprits are snails, slugs, and, occasionally, earwigs. Thrips rarely invade the container garden, especially if you're using "artificial soils." Snails and slugs are about the easiest of all garden pests to control in a container garden if you stay one step ahead of them.

The foliage of the bulbs is usually unappetizing to the regular pests. If a problem does appear, it's easy for you to remedy it, as you would with other plants in containers.

This Chinese ('Meyer') lemon is a relatively old dwarf variety, excellent for containers.

FRUIT IN CONTAINERS

Fruit trees make decorative container plants and also can provide a delicious harvest.

Fruit trees have been grown in containers for a long time. One of the most famous container-fruit gardens belonged to Louis XIV, who, in the 1600s, had an orangerie constructed at Versailles. The orangerie was the predecessor of the modern greenhouse, and tender trees could be grown in it to produce fruit out of season. Some of the fruit trees at Versailles are said to have lasted 75 years.

You, however, don't need to think or work on such a grand scale as at Versailles to keep a container orchard. The development of modern dwarfing techniques has considerably reduced the work required (dwarf trees are far less likely to get rootbound or cause problems with watering and feeding). Dwarf trees, both grafted and natural, are discussed in detail later in this chapter; but first, here are some step-by-step planting and maintenance techniques that will keep your portable orchard healthy and productive for years.

Climate Considerations

As the Versailles garden shows, planting in containers will allow even tender plants far from their natural climate zone to grow well; you can move them to shelter when cold weather comes, or wheel them to a shady spot if it gets too hot.

Containers give you no excuse not to try 'Meyer' lemons in Michigan or peaches in North Dakota. Choose a winter holding-site that has plenty of light but not too much heat. Be careful not to overwater while the plants are inactive. Citrus is decorative enough to be brought into the house and put in front of a south window, but put deciduous material in the garage—it will probably survive a season there, as long as you get it out into the sun on fine spring days.

One warning: just because a plant can survive winter in the ground doesn't mean that it can manage cold weather in a container. If your garden soil freezes, then container soil definitely will freeze and your plants will die. Plants in containers do not have the protective insulation of the soil that plants in the ground do. If you live in the coldest northern zones, protect even hardy deciduous plants in the coldest months.

What Plants To Choose

Our variety lists and the pages on dwarf trees will give you more extensive information on plants that suit containers. For now, here are just a few ideas: apples on Malling 7, 9, or 26 dwarfing rootstocks; pears on quince roots; genetic dwarf peaches, nectarines, apricot, or cherry; any fig; the smaller crabapples; citrus on trifoliate orange roots, where available; strawberries; and spur-pruned grape varieties. When the new Malling 27 rootstock becomes widely available for apples, it should be ideal for container planting.

Size of Container

Begin your container orchard with containers that are just two or three inches wider than the roots of your plants. If you start with a bare-root apple or pear

or a genetic dwarf fruit, your first container should be about the size of a 5-gallon lard can. In fact, since it will only be in use for one growing season, you might actually use a lard can, covering it with a basket or box to disguise it. Let the young tree grow for a season and fill the container with roots; then repot it the following spring.

Evergreen fruit plants such as citrus should start out in a container that's not too much bigger than their rootball. If your soil mix is well drained, you can go to a box three or four inches wider than the roots all around. With large nursery plants, the first container may be the last.

Permanent containers should be no bigger than bushel-basket size—anything larger will be too bulky to handle or move, although you might consider a platform on wheels for any large container. Half barrels are about the right size; so is any box or pot that holds about that volume of soil. Permanent containers should be no smaller than about 18 inches on a side and 18 inches deep. The smaller the container, the more work is involved in feeding, watering, and root pruning.

A container that can be taken apart is most practical. You can attach one side with screws; better yet, you can screw all four sides together for easy removal. Container trees must be removed from their pots every two or three years for root pruning (see sketches on page 31). Otherwise all the feeder roots will bunch at the walls of the container and the plant will languish.

Move plants from the first (5-gallon size) container to the bushel size over two or three seasons. When a plant has the appropriate-size container, it can find water and nutrients easily. The right size also keeps soil from going sour around and beneath the roots, and slows top growth.

Container Soil Mix

Some gardeners like to add a little rich loam to the mix of sand and organic material. It holds water better and helps keep nutrients available. Add up to ⅓ loam if you like, but be careful not to include clay soil. It holds water too well for a container mix, and you may drown your plants. With a purely synthetic mix (see discussion of synthetic soils, page 22), be careful about feeding: the nutrients you add leach away when you water. Keep to a regular schedule, as outlined below.

Feeding Container Fruit

Let the growth of the plant and its general appearance determine your feeding schedule. The plant should leaf out and grow vigorously in the spring and early summer, and the leaves should be a healthy medium green. Yellowed leaves suggest a lack of nitrogen; very dark leaves may mean you're feeding too much.

One method of feeding is to give each plant about half the recommended quantity of complete fertilizer (containing nitrogen, phosphoric acid, and potassium or potash) about every two to three weeks rather than the full amount once a month. A liquid fertilizer is easy to handle and less likely to burn roots. If the directions say 1 tablespoon per gallon of water, use half that amount (1½ teaspoons) instead, and fertilize twice as often.

You can also use one of the pelleted slow-release fertilizers. Since these dissolve slowly over a period of time, they won't wash away in the first week or so.

Feed through the growing season if the plant is to receive winter protection. Stop about mid-July if it is to stay outdoors. That will give it a chance to harden up new growth.

A note of caution: when drainage is poor, fertilizer can build up in a pot and begin to burn the plant. If you see brown, dry-looking leaf edges, water heavily as described in the following section on watering. This heavy watering (leaching) will clean the soil.

Citrus requires about the same amount of feeding as deciduous fruit, but it may also require a few extra nutrients. Special citrus foods containing iron, zinc, and sometimes other minerals are available at nurseries. Use them regularly, or switch to them if you see leaves with yellowed portions between bright

green veins. If the leaf is uniformly yellow, veins and all, the plant lacks nitrogen. Citrus food also can be used on deciduous plants without harming them, but it may cost more than deciduous plant food.

Here are some possibilities for container-grown fruiting plants. They can grow indoors or out depending on your climate, but any of them can produce year-round fruit in greenhouses. Beginning at top left and reading clockwise: Ponderosa lemons; a red-leafed dwarf banana tree; an orange tree from the Palace at Versailles; strawberries in a wooden hanging basket; tart tangerines; and peaches.

Watering Container Fruits

Judge the amount of watering your plant needs by its behavior. It should never wilt, but neither should it stand in soggy soil. If you check the soil occasionally by digging down an inch or two, you'll soon learn how much to water. The top inch may stay moist for a week in fairly cool weather; however, when the weather is hot and windy, water frequently—perhaps even every day for a plant that needs repotting. Frequent watering is why well-drained soil is so important—you can pour on the water without drowning the roots.

Mulch will help keep the soil moist and cool. Use a coarse organic mulch such as bark chips, and pile it about 2 inches thick. In really hot weather, group your containers—it will help conserve moisture and provide partial shade.

Don't count on rain to do all your watering, since plants in containers may act as umbrellas and shed most of the rain. Check the soil even when rainfall has

Two suggestions for containers with trellises that can be used for grapes: on the left, two grape plants are trained across two pairs of wire cross supports. See page 138 for construction information. On the right, an unusual-shaped container with trellises that accentuate that shape. See page 140 for construction information.

been abundant. Rain will enable you to water less often, however—the moist air will keep water from evaporating.

You'll need to leach the soil occasionally. Leaching is a long soaking that dissolves any minerals or salts and flushes them out the drain hole. Well water, or any water that leaves bathtub rings or doesn't produce good soapsuds, is heavy with dissolved mineral salts, which remain and accumulate in container soil as water evaporates. Eventually you'll see brown leaf edges, then dead leaves, and finally a dead plant. To avoid disaster, put your garden hose in each container every couple of months and let it run slowly for about 20 minutes, or just long enough to allow the water to go through the soil and out the drainhole. Don't let it overflow, however.

If yours is a hard-water area, for every watering fill the pot until water runs freely from the bottom. Go on to other pots, then return and fill the first pot and then the other ones a second time. This technique keeps salts to a minimum.

Vacation watering. When you leave home, group your containers near a water source out of the afternoon sun. The grouping will help keep them moist; the shade will cut the need for water; and, if they're near a hose, none will be overlooked by your vacation waterer. For large numbers of containers, you can buy water timers that will turn water on at regular intervals. Just hook up a system of small hoses that you place permanently in each container. Commercial drip systems are effective here too, provided you filter the water before it goes into the system. Filtering is necessary because the drip openings are small and easily clogged. Filters can be bought at most garden centers.

Potting and Repotting

There are many successful potting methods, and gardeners have great success with methods you'll never see recommended in books (except this one). These suggestions should work every time and keep your plants healthy.

The ideal is a container soil that holds water but never gets soggy. Water should soak in immediately, not sit on top, and should run out just as fast. Choose a synthetic soil or a mixture of synthetic soil and garden loam. Moisten the soil until it's barely damp but not wet. You may find it best to sprinkle and stir the soil one day, then pot your plants the next.

Be sure your pot or box has good drainage holes. If you buy a container with one small hole, drill two or three more, or ask the nurseryman to do it for you. If you're planning to use a can for a season, first punch a dozen holes around the bottom with a beer can opener. Cover the holes with broken pieces of pot or broken crockery. The soil mix should fill the pot from top to bottom.

Place enough soil mix in the pot, lightly tamped down, so that the roots touch it when the crown of the plant is just below the pot rim. Hold your bare-root plant at that level and toss in enough soil to support it, tamping lightly as you go. Then finish filling to about ¼ inch below the pot rim. The soil will settle, leaving you room to water. For an evergreen plant, or any plant in a nursery container, simply place it on the first layer of soil, then fill around it. However, before covering the rootball, scratch it all around with a fork to roughen up the roots and get them pointing outward. Cut off any long, spiraling roots at the bottom of the rootball.

To repot, use a similar technique (described in the illustrations here). Repotting is necessary because any plant tends to bunch feeder roots at the wall of the container, where they dry out faster. Even when cared for properly, a potted plant eventually will need more water and nutrients than it can get in a pot it has been in too long. Shaving off an inch of root and adding fresh soil will allow the plant to grow healthy young roots and will give the empty soil around them a reservoir of moisture. Always clip the top back a little when you shave off the roots to balance the plant. New top growth will follow the new root growth.

After potting and repotting, soak the soil thoroughly.

These half-barrels are ideal containers for 'Southern Sweet' genetic dwarf peaches. There is even room for a little annual color below.

Citrus Fruit

Growing your own citrus fruit will certainly seem worthwhile when you breakfast on homegrown oranges, but the dwarf trees described here do have conditions to be met. They need: direct sun at least half of every bright winter day; comfortable room temperatures; and moist, humusy soil (equal parts of garden loam, peat moss, and sand). Feed with a liquid house-plant food every 2 to 4 weeks, and give the plants a shower with tepid water once a month. Keep outdoors during frost-free weather.

Invest only in dwarf varieties developed specifically for pot culture. These will produce fragrant flowers all year, as well as edible fruit. If leaf yellowing occurs, correct by using a fertilizer labeled for acid-loving plants.

To produce fruit indoors, you may need to emulate the bee and do some pollinating. With an artist's brush, transfer pollen from the stamen of one flower to the stigma (the pistil end protruding beyond the petals) of another.

'Washington' naval orange

Calamondin (*Citrofortunella mitis*). This dwarf citrus will produce abundant 1- to 2-inch, orange-like fruits every month of the year. Leave them on the tree to brighten your surroundings, or use them to make marmalade.

Otaheite Orange (*Citrus* × *limonia*). A miniature version of the sweet orange, this plant produces 1- to 2-inch fruits. However, they taste more like a lime than an orange. They will remain on the tree for as long as two years.

Meyer or Chinese Lemon (*Citrus limon* 'Meyer'). This dwarf tree is a relatively old variety, bearing flowers that range in color from lavender to white, followed by bright yellow lemons. These are excellent for cooking.

Ponderosa Lemon (*Citrus limon* 'Ponderosa'). Probably the most spectacular of the dwarf citruses, this one has glossy green leaves, sharp spines, and lemons that weigh from one to three pounds. Each one takes about six months to mature, but this plant will have fruit at varying stages of maturity, year-round. When fruits reach maturity, you will need to prop the branches with stakes.

In summer and warm-climate regions you can grow oranges in outdoor containers. In cooler areas they work quite well in sunny windows.

Left: A container and trellis especially designed for espaliering. See page 138 for construction details.
Below: The edible fig *Ficus carica*. Its dwarf forms adapt best to indoor/outdoor mobility.

Persian Lime (*Citrus aurantiifolia* 'Tahiti'). For full-sized limes, this is the dwarf citrus to grow. The fruits are bright chartreuse-green, and the plant is easily kept under two feet high.

Other dwarf citruses available are grapefruit, limequat, tangelo, citron, tangerine, and Nagami kumquat.

Fruiting Pot Plants

Here are more ornamentals—some with edible fruit—that are easy to grow in pots.

Coffee (*Coffea arabica*). Large shiny leaves, fragrant white flowers, and bright red berries make this tree of interest.

Dwarf Bananas (species of *Musa*). A must for every plant lover. These graceful ornamentals have wide green leaves contrasted with brightly colored bracts and fruit. During the Victorian era in Europe, it was referred to as "table banana" because the entire potted plant was used to decorate banquet tables.

Dwarf Pomegranate (*Punica granatum* 'Nana'). Delicate red flowers grow on branches of pale green leaves in summer. Tiny edible fruits appear in autumn. Another variety (*P.* 'Chico') does not bear fruit, but has 1-inch, orange, carnation-like flowers.

Edible Fig (*Ficus carica*). Varieties produce green, yellow, or purplish fruit. It is among the easiest deciduous fruit trees to grow. Plant in a large tub with ordinary garden soil, give it sun, and keep it moist during the growing season. In cold climates, the trees will need complete winter protection. Dwarf forms are available, making seasonal mobility easier.

A good crop from plastic pails sunk in the ground. The ground is covered with shredded fir bark.

When you crowd plants in containers, compensate for lack of root space with frequent light liquid feeding.

The strawberry adapts well to container planting, in pots, boxes, or baskets—hanging or otherwise.

Natal Plum 'Fancy' (*Carissa grandiflora*). This hybrid bears white, star-like flowers and red, cranberry-flavored fruit that can be used to make a fine jelly.

Pineapple Guava (*Feijoa sellowiana*). This bears spectacular 1- to 2-inch red flowers, and green, edible fruit on a small evergreen tree or shrub. Root it from cuttings during warm weather (needs high humidity) in sand or perlite. Then grow in loamy soil with plenty of sand and humus.

Pyracantha 'Red Elf' (*Pyracantha coccinea*). Clusters of vivid scarlet berries grow in autumn and winter. Though the berries are inedible, they make this bushy plant a most attractive container plant.

South American Tree Tomato (*Cyphomandra betacea*). Delicious, egg-shaped, red fruits are sweeter than ordinary tomatoes and excellent for making jams.

Other fruiting plants. The following will thrive in containers: dwarf pineapple; Surinam cherry (*Eugenia*); the tea of commerce (*Thea sinensis*); cherry tomatoes, such as 'Tiny Tim'; bush pepper (*Piper magnificum*); Christmas pepper (*Capsicum annuum*); and the runnerless strawberries, such as 'Catherine', 'Baron Solemacher', and the variegated form, *Fragaria vesca* 'Albo-marginata'.

Strawberries in Containers

You can grow strawberries in hanging baskets, in clay and wooden strawberry barrels, in 5-gallon plastic pails, in planter boxes, and along walls.

For maximum production, the container should be large enough to nourish a root system that's at least 8 inches wide and 8 inches deep. Restricting the root system in too small a container reduces production; reducing any part of the root system affects the entire plant.

Instead of planting 8 crowns, try planting only 4 plants to the 48-inch-long planter box. You may get more berries over a longer time. Soil should be fairly rich with organic matter and should drain well. Don't set the plants too high in the soil, or the top part of the roots will dry out. Similarly, don't set the crown of the plant below the surface of the soil or it will rot.

If you're using a disease-free soil mix, you don't have to worry about verticillium wilt and red stele (root rot), since both are caused by soil-borne fungi. It's best to start with plants certified to be virus-free. In general, these will outproduce other varieties and will bear good crops for up to three years or more.

The performance of strawberries from year to year is not exactly predictable. The quality of the same variety may differ from one year to the next due to differences in the weather pattern and soil conditions. Also, the "best" variety in one location may be only fair in another. Varieties available at local garden centers are adapted to your area, but you can also check with the office of your County Agricultural Extension Agent for suggested varieties.

Here are some of the recommended varieties:

Standard varieties. 'Armore'. Late midseason. Large berries of good flavor are yellowish-red outside, lighter inside. Prolific in heavy silt loam.

'Cyclone'. Early. Large, delicious berries are good for freezing. Plant is winter hardy and resistant to foliage diseases.

'Surecrop'. Early. This large, round, glossy, firm variety is of good dessert quality. Space large plants 6 to 9 inches apart for top production. Resistant to red stele, verticillium wilt, leaf spots, leaf scorch, and drought.

Everbearing varieties. 'Geneva'. Produces large, vigorous plants that fruit well in June and throughout the summer and early autumn. Berries are soft and very highly flavored.

'Ogallala'. Medium-sized berries are dark red, soft, and tasty. Good for freezing. Vigorous grower. Hardy.

'Ozark Beauty'. Large, sweet, tasty berries are bright red outside and inside. Production occurs on mother plants, but not on runner plants during summer and fall.

A strawberry "tree" is a half-cylinder of wire mesh filled with soil mix that is held in position by sphagnum moss. Impatiens add color at the bottom. (See page 127.)

Vegetables can be part of a bigger scheme. Here tomatoes share a container with alyssum.

VEGETABLES IN CONTAINERS

Even city dwellers can have a vegetable garden if they use containers.

When you grow vegetables in containers, you can take advantage of the various micro-climates around the house and garden. You might plant the heat-loving eggplant in a spot where it gets not only full sunlight but also the reflected heat off a south wall.

You can use all sizes of pots, cans, plastic buckets, plastic trash containers, garbage cans, bulb pots, azalea pots, fiber pots, paint buckets, half whiskey-barrels, and fruit baskets (peck and bushel).

The larger the container, the more soil you'll need. A large amount of soil allows the plant roots to draw on a reserve of moisture and nutrients. It is easier to water and feed plants in large containers than in small containers, since the latter require more frequent care. However, suit your container to the plant; it doesn't make sense to give a plant a soil depth of 16 or 18 inches if it can produce in a container of 6 to 8 inches deep.

When gardening on a balcony or roof, you must consider the weight of the containers for the sake of safety. Too great a weight might make the balcony or roof collapse. To get 50 square feet of planting space with 16-inch-deep containers, you need 67 cubic feet of soil mix. If the containers or boxes are 8 inches deep, you'd need only half that amount of soil.

Container Size and Capacity

There is no such thing as a standard-size container except for old clay pots, which graduate uniformly from 2 to 16 inches.

A gallon-size container is described by different manufacturers as 7¼″ × 6¼″, 7½″ × 7½″, and 6¼″ × 7″. The dimensions indicate diameter by depth. The thickness of the material—fiber, metal, type of plastic—and the *taper* of the pot accounts for the difference of the dimensions.

Sizes of containers by gallons:

1 gallon—7¼″ × 6¼″	3 gallon—10″ × 10″	5 gallon—12″ × 12″
2 gallon—8″ × 8″	4 gallon—12″ × 11″	6 gallon—13″ × 13″

Sizes of standard redwood octagonal planter tubs:

12″ × 11″   14″ × 12½″   16″ × 14″   18″ × 15″

A Productive Container Garden

With a substantial vegetable harvest as a goal, the following plan for a patio or balcony garden has been worked out to show the kind of container-crop yield possible.

After a year of experimenting, test gardeners settled on three types of containers:

For onions, carrots, beets, turnips, kohlrabi, and zucchini, they used 24″ × 36″ boxes, 8 inches deep.

Above: A test to determine the minimum-size container required for various vegetables.
Right: The Ball Company, supplier to bedding plant growers, demonstrates productivity of tomatoes, eggplants, peppers, and cucumbers, grown in Jiffy tubs.

For pole beans, cucumbers, and peas, they used a narrow 12″ × 48″ box, 8 inches deep. Many also built a trellis for training these vegetables to grow vertically.

For peppers, eggplant, and tomatoes, they preferred the single 4- and 5-gallon containers.

Typical plantings in the 24″ × 36″ box included: four rows of carrots, 5 inches apart, thinned to 3 inches apart in the row; and two rows of onion sets for green onions, set 2 inches apart in the row. (See notes on these vegetables in the following individual vegetable list and in the illustration below.)

Many gardeners assume that all vegetables require full sunlight, but many vegetables will tolerate filtered shade. According to the USDA Home and Garden Bulletin No. 163, *Minigardens for Vegetables:*

"Vegetable plants grow better in full sunlight than in shade. Some vegetables need more sun than others. Leafy vegetables (lettuce, cabbage, mustard greens) can stand more shade than root vegetables (beets, radishes, turnips). Root vegetables can stand more shade than vegetable fruit plants (cucumbers, peppers, tomatoes), which do very poorly in the shade. Plant your fruiting vegetable plants where they will get the most sun and your leafy vegetables and root vegetables in the shadier areas."

The suggestions for the sizes of the containers indicate whether it's the 24″ × 36″ box or the 12″ × 48″ box or a 2-, 3-, 4-, or 5- gallon container. You don't have to keep to these dimensions—the recommendations are made only to emphasize the box's width or narrowness.

Container Garden Production

The containers in this garden would take up less than 75 square feet of patio, deck, or balcony space. One way to arrange all of these on a 6′ × 20′ balcony is shown at lower right. A plan for a 6′ × 10′ container garden is at lower left.

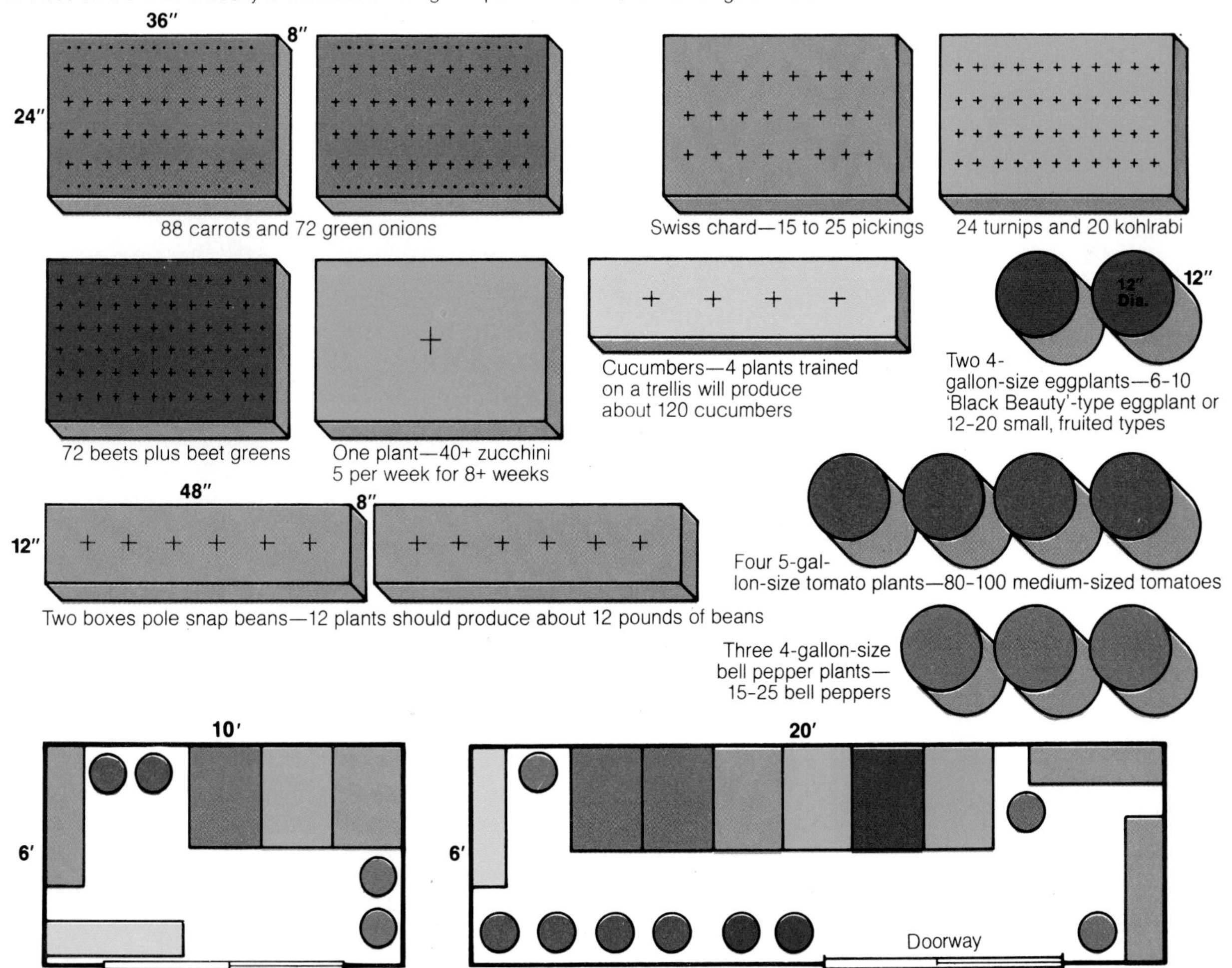

This simple, easy-to-construct box holds carrots (above) and beets (right). See page 131 for construction details.

The Vegetables

Beets.

Season: Cool, early, and late.
Light: Tolerates partial shade.
Spacing: 2 to 3 inches apart in row.
Container: 24″ × 36″ × 8″ box.
Harvest: When 1 to 2 inches in diameter.
Comments: Take plants when 6 to 8 inches high. Use thinnings for greens. Favorite varieties: 'Golden Beet' (55 days). Tops taste better than spinach when boiled as greens. 'Detroit Dark Red' (60 days), round shape.

Beets actually produce two crops—first the thinnings, or "greens," then the mature harvest.

Carrots

Season: Spring, early summer, fall.
Light: Tolerates partial shade.
Spacing: 1½ to 3 inches in the row. Thin early to avoid tangled roots.
Container: 24″ × 36″ × 10″ box. Loose, deep soil is required.
Harvest: For small carrots, harvest when ½ to 1 inch in diameter.
Comments: Plant for succession. Choose short-rooted varieties, such as 'Nantes Half Long' (70 days), with cylindrical roots 6 to 7 inches long; 'Royal Chantenay' (70 days), broad shouldered, with 4- to 7-inch roots.

Above: Large cucumbers hang from an A-frame wood trellis. They take less ground space when trained this way and are easy to pick.

Chives

Season: A hardy perennial.
Light: Grow in partial shade, as in a kitchen window.
Spacing: 2 to 3 inches (in clusters).
Container: 4-inch pot.
Harvest: Clip as needed. If not clipped, chives produce attractive lavender flower heads.
Comments: For a quick harvest, buy plants. Small clumps spread rapidly. Divide chives occasionally so they don't get too thick.

Cucumbers

Season: Warm summer.
Light: Require full sunlight.
Spacing: 12 to 16 inches in 48-inch box.
Container: 12″ × 48″ × 8″ box with trellis.
Harvest: Pick before hard seeds form.
Comments: A great many varieties. Train the strong vining types on a trellis. One plant will produce 20 to 30 fruits. The bush type, such as 'Patio Pik' and 'Salty', produce on vines only 18 to 24 inches long.

Left and below: Designed for growing vine crops vertically, this A-frame trellis has lemon cucumbers on one side and beans on the other. See page 129 for construction details.

Right: Eggplants will probably need support when they bear fruit.
Below: Kale mixed with flowering annuals.

Eggplant
Season: Warm summer.
Light: Needs full sunlight.
Spacing: One plant to a container.
Container: 4- to 5-gallon size.
Harvest: At any stage from ⅓ to ⅔ their normal mature size. Good fruit has a high gloss.
Comments: Choose early varieties such as 'Mission Bell' in short-season areas. Standard varieties require high heat and a long growing season. In containers, the varieties with medium- to small-sized fruits carried high on the plant are more interesting than the lower-growing, heavy-fruited varieties.

Kale
Season: Grows best in cool days of fall. Flavor improved by frost.
Light: Tolerates partial shade
Spacing: 6 inches.
Container: Plant in 12″ × 48″ box.
Harvest: When tall enough for greens; cut whole plants or take larger leaves.
Comments: Grows to 12 to 18 inches tall and as wide. The leaves of the variety 'Blue Curled Scotch' are as curled as parsley.

Leeks
Season: Winter hardy. 130 to 150 days from seed. 80 to 90 days from transplants.
Light: Tolerates partial shade.
Spacing: 2 to 3 inches in the row.
Container: Grow in 24″ × 36″ box.
Harvest: When 1 inch in diameter and white part is 5 to 6 inches long.
Comments: Leeks do not form bulbs as onions do. The thickened stems can be blanched by hilling soil around them.

Lettuce
Season: Early spring or fall.
Light: Tolerates partial shade.
Spacing: Leaf lettuce 4 to 6 inches. Head lettuce 10 inches.
Container: Head lettuce: give it room—space 10 inches apart in the row. Use 24″ × 36″ box, or 12″ × 48″ box. Leaf lettuce: any container will do. Can be harvested as it grows, leaf by leaf.
Comments: High temperatures and long days cause lettuce to flower (bolt). For all but early spring and fall plantings, choose varieties that are slow to bolt, such as 'Summer Bibb', 'Buttercrunch', 'Oakleaf', and 'Slobolt'.

The depth of the box is the critical measurement. Recommended depths for various vegetables are shown on page 99. Once you actually are ready to have container grown vegetables showing in your garden, though, it's nice to match the plant with the container. On the left, the 'Ruby Ball' cabbage and the 'Bibb' lettuce seem well placed in this rounded tub.

Right: 'Rhubarb Chard' is a colorful addition to any garden. The leaves are milder tasting and more tender than other varieties.
Below: Green onion.

Onions (green)
Season: Plant sets in early spring and in September.
Light: Green onions grow in partial shade; mature bulbs need full sun.
Spacing: 2 inches in the row.
Container: Any container 6 inches or more deep.
Harvest: When 8 to 10 inches tall.
Comments: Leave one green onion every 4 inches or so to form a bulb. The small bulbs are usable as cooked onions after they dry out.

Parsley
Season: Cool. A biennial—produces foliage the first year, and goes to seed the next spring. Treat as an annual.
Light: Does well in partial shade. Will grow on kitchen windowsills.
Spacing: 6 to 8 inches in the row in a box.
Container: 4-inch pot indoors.
Harvest: Clip for garnish.
Comments: For garnishing, the variety 'Moss Curled', also called 'Extra Curled Dwarf', is the standard curled-leaf variety. For flavoring, the "plain" or "single" is the standard variety. The 'Hamburg Rooted' is grown for its parsnip-like roots 6 inches or longer and about 2 inches thick at the neck.

Peppers
Season: Warm summer.
Light: Require full sunlight.
Spacing: 14 to 18 inches apart in row in a box.
Container: Allow one plant per 2- to 4-gallon container.
Harvest: Harvest bell peppers when 2 to 3 inches in diameter.
Comments: Almost any variety, hot or sweet, is worth displaying on patio or deck for its ornamental value—shiny green leaves, small white flowers, and fruits in many shapes and colors (green, yellow, and red).

Potatoes
Season: Late spring, early summer.
Light: Require full sunlight.
Spacing: 2 seed pieces to the container.
Container: 5-gallon size or larger.

Harvest: When tops die down.
Comments: Plant seed pieces ¾ the way down in the container, adding a mulch-type soil as the potatoes grow, so you can "pick" rather than dig the potatoes.

Swiss Chard
Season: Spring, summer, fall.
Light: Tolerates partial shade.
Spacing: 4 to 5 inches in the row; 6 inches between rows.
Container: Any container 6 to 8 inches deep.
Harvest: When leaves are 3 inches or more in length.
Comments: Only one planting is needed. Outer leaves may be harvested without injury to the plant. A great "cut and come again" plant.

Some vegetables, potatoes for instance, will thrive in almost any container that gives them enough room. Reading clockwise from top left we see potatoes being harvested from a peck fruit basket; growing in the same basket; being watered in a plastic trash bag; and being harvested from a plastic garbage container.

Top: This adjustable trellis can be widened to train two or more plants or adjusted to fit one pot in less space. See page 136 for construction details.
Above: Another good trellis box for tomatoes. See page 139 for construction details.

Tomatoes

Season: Poor fruit set when night temperatures are below 60°F. or above 75°F. Need 3 to 4 months of temperatures in the 65° to 85°F. range.
Light: Require full sunlight at least 6 hours a day.
Spacing: Depends on variety and how trained.
Container: Give the strong, large-fruited varieties a 4- to 5-gallon-sized container. See below for sizes of container varieties.
Comments: There are hundreds of varieties. Check your nurseryman or County Extension Agent for varieties adapted to your area. A number of varieties especially suited for container growing have been introduced in the last few years. If you are using garden soil or compost in your soil mix, you should favor the disease-resistant varieties. Resistance is indicated by the initials "V"—Verticillium; "F"—Fusarium; "N"—Nematode. (Using sterilized soil mixes of peat moss and vermiculite or perlite will help you avoid soil-borne diseases—see page 22.)

Varieties: 'Atom' (*60 days*)—Heavy production of small, 1-inch fruits. Well adapted to indoor growing in 8- to 10-inch pots, or hanging baskets.

Burpee's 'Early Salad Hybrid' (*45 days*)—Compact plants grow only 6 to 8 inches high with a spread of about 2 feet. One plant will produce from 250 to 300 fruits measuring 1½ to 1¾ inches.

Burpee's 'Pixie Hybrid' (*55 days*)—Grows 14 to 18 inches tall. Fruits 1¾ inches. Grow in 8-inch pot or hanging basket. Will produce indoors in winter in sunny window.

'Patio Hybrid' F (*70 days*)—Extra-sturdy main stem is like the trunk of a small tree. Grows to about 30 inches. Needs no staking until heavy with its 2-inch fruit. Best in a 12-inch tub or pot.

'Presto' (*60 days*)—The small-leaved, rather open vine grows to about 2 feet tall with a heavy yield of half-dollar-sized fruits. Grow in a 3- to 5-gallon container and support it with a short stake.

'Small Fry' VF (*55 days*)—Similar to 'Atom' in growth habit. Vigorous grower to 30 inches, bearing 1-inch fruits in profusion. Best in a 12-inch pot or box with trellis. Beautiful in a hanging basket.

'Stakeless' F (*78 days*)—Similar to 'Patio' in sturdy growth habit. Dense foliage. Grows 20 to 24 inches tall with 5- to 8-ounce (2-inch and larger) fruits. Plant in a 10- to 12-inch pot.

'Tiny Tim' (*55 days from transplant*)—The midget of the group. Only 15 inches tall with ¾-inch scarlet fruit. Give it a 6-inch pot or hanging basket, or plant two in an 8-inch pot.

'Tumblin' Tom' VFN (*48 days*)—A new introduction in the hanging-basket class. Heavy yield of 1½- to 2-inch fruits. Vine grows 20 to 24 inches tall.

Left: These interwoven lath panels are supported by portable posts in clay pots. The panel hides the container. See page 137 for construction detail.
Below: A simple trellis added to a planter box supports a 'Small Fry' tomato crop.

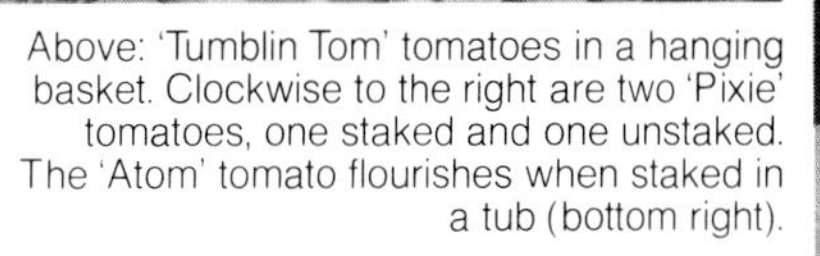

Above: 'Tumblin Tom' tomatoes in a hanging basket. Clockwise to the right are two 'Pixie' tomatoes, one staked and one unstaked. The 'Atom' tomato flourishes when staked in a tub (bottom right).

Top: Waist-high raised beds make gardening easier on your back and brings everything into view.
Above: Turnips and beets eventually require the same soil and nutrients to grow properly.

Turnips
Season: Cool. Plant 4 to 6 weeks before last frost in spring and 6 to 8 weeks before first fall freeze.
Light: Tolerate partial shade.
Spacing: Thin when large enough to make greens and leave others to mature.
Container: Try combining them with kohlrabi in a 24″ × 36″ box, and harvest both when small.
Comments: 'Tokyo Cross' is a good variety, but so are all the others when picked small.

Zucchini
Season: Warm summer.
Light: Does best in full sunlight.
Spacing: One plant per 5-gallon container.
Container: Larger than 12 inches in diameter. Use the 24″ × 36″ box.
Harvest: When 1½ to 2 inches in diameter.
Comments: One plant will produce 6 or more fruits a week.

Herbs. A box 12″ × 48″ × 8″ deep will serve well as a patio herb garden. Chives, garden thyme, basil, marjoram, and summer savory will do well in the confines of this planter box. The sprawling growth habit of the various mints and oregano makes them attractive in hanging baskets. If you have room for 12-inch pots or tubs, you can add these to your herb list: tarragon, winter savory, rosemary, and a young sweet bay tree.

It's easy to set a stage for a collection of potted herbs and flowering plants. Here weathered boxes make the stage multilevel.

Hung to receive filtered light, the cascading blossoms of this *Epiphyllum* 'Duchess Kaiserine' hybrid are a striking display.

SUCCULENTS IN CONTAINERS

Succulents come in a wide variety of colors, shapes, textures, and sizes, and they make excellent and interesting container plants.

The fascinating world of succulents offers an astounding and varied range. It includes nearly all cacti as well as many members of the lily family, the daisy family, and the bromeliad family.

Succulents are the camels of the plant kingdom; they too have devised some very clever water-conservation techniques to carry them through periods of drought. Some are disguised to look like stones to avoid being eaten by animals.

Unlike desert cacti, not all succulents are arid-area types. Some come from tropical areas where long, dry seasons are followed by a short season of heavy rains that leave the air moist but the terrain dry. These areas gave birth to such tropical cacti as *Rhipsalis* and *Epiphyllum* ("Orchid cactus"). The lily family includes such succulent members as the well known aloes (*A. vera* is popular as a skin treatment for burns); the elephant foot tree or ponytail from Mexico, *Beaucarnea recurvata;* and the many *Sansevieria* species (Mother-in-law's tongue). These are but a few among thousands of succulents.

Basics for Container Growing

Succulents make interesting and relatively easy-to-grow container plants. Different succulent plants have their own individual preferences, and if you follow these basic suggestions you should have success with them.

Choosing a container. Drainage is the most important factor to consider when you are selecting a container. For most succulents, a clay pot just large enough to accommodate the plant without overcrowding its roots is best. If you put a small plant in too large a pot, it won't be able to absorb the water quickly enough, and rot may occur. Bonsai containers do a splendid job of displaying succulents, and their drainage holes are ideal. Use a fiberglass windowscreen mesh (obtainable in hardware stores or garden centers) to cover holes so your potting soil won't spill through.

Most succulents need to dry out between waterings, which is another good reason to choose a clay pot over plastic or any other nonporous material. Clay and other porous materials let you control the wet/dry needs of your succulents more easily. However, this doesn't mean you should never plant a succulent in a plastic pot; a plastic container does require less frequent watering, which is especially useful when you're on vacation.

Watering. Like any other plants, succulents should have rain water or bottled water rather than tap water. The quality of the water is important. Succulents are sensitive to salt, which exists in large amounts in the water of certain areas, as well as in softened water, which should never be used to water any plants. Accumulated salts in the root area cripple growth and cause eventual death. To leach accumulated salts from the root area, about every fourth watering fill the pot with water from the top and let drain. Repeat this three times.

During their growing season, succulents should be watered whenever the

1

2

3

4

soil has begun to dry out. During their period of rest, however, hold back on watering. Most succulents are sensitive to being wet when the weather is cold. In late fall when the temperatures begin to drop, dole out the water sparingly, just enough to keep the roots alive. A turkey baster is handy for fall or winter watering when you need to provide just enough to maintain the roots and avoid wilting. For days at a stretch in winter, sometimes all you need to do is mist the surface of the soil and wet the outside of the pot (use an ordinary plastic spray bottle).

Don't allow the foliage to get limp and shriveled before you water. Learn to observe your plants—you will soon be able to tell when they want water or when they want to rest. Some of your succulents will need to be watered less frequently than others; not all will need to rest as early or for as long as others. By watching closely, getting to know them better, and understanding their responses, you will begin to react to their needs automatically.

When night temperatures begin to rise and the plant begins to show signs of fresh growth, it's time to begin normal, thorough watering again. Set the pots in a pan of water and allow them to "drink" until the soil is just moist on top.

Potting soil. Succulents need an open, well-drained mix. Although all (including the desert cacti) are said to "require" a lean mix (low in nutritive content), experienced specialists agree that most succulent plants in cultivation prefer a fairly rich soil mix. Most tropical succulents (see selection guide, page 116) prefer acid soil; others (the arid-region species) like a slightly alkaline soil. This acid-alkalinity factor may be controlled by soil additives (see container soils, page 22).

Fertilizing. Fertilize succulents *only during the growing period.* Never fertilize with more than a quarter to a third of the recommended dilution printed on the

1. Colorful *Echeveria* hybrid 'Meridian'. 2. *Aichryson laxum* from the Canary Islands. 3. Silvery succulents *(Dudleya subrigida* and *D. brittoni)* stand out in this collection. 4. Hen-and-chickens *(Sempervivum)* in a vertical planter. 5. This staging of succulents includes *Oscularia deltoides*, lower left, with assorted *Crassulaceae*. 6. This Medusa's head *(Euphorbia caput-medusae)* has been made to live up to its name.

5

6

1. 'Ghost Plant' *(Graptopetalum paraguayense)* in a ceramic lady's head. 2. The centers of the clay baskets are planted with *Echeveria elegans* circled by *Senecio serpens*. 3. Donkey tail *(Sedum morganianum)* drapes from hanging pots. 4. Sedum grows with very little soil and adapts well to many types of rock plantings.

package directions. It is always better to feed in small, frequent amounts—about every third watering. Stop all feeding as soon as the plants cease to show further seasonal growth. Never feed during their resting period.

Air temperature and light. Good air circulation is crucial to the health of your succulents. Stagnant air encourages mealybugs on any "dry-growing" plant. All succulents (even the desert cacti) like early morning humidity, but evaporation must take place to remove any excess moisture within a short period. A most cooperative example is the morning dew that freshens foliage and disappears with the warming rays of the morning sun (for some succulents, this is the only moisture they will receive for months at a time in their native habitat). Your succulents should not have wet leaves at night. Keep them cool (not cold) at night, and let the full sun warm them during the day (unless, like the tropical cacti, they prefer filtered sun). They will respond exuberantly to your care.

Few succulents tolerate frost. Plan to give them winter protection with as much sunlight as possible.

As shade plants, succulents can do remarkable things. The ice plant, for instance, makes a fine green hanging basket. True ice plant (*Mesembryanthemum crystallinum* of the Aizoaceae family) always has an icy, "beaded" appearance, like moisture formed on a container of frozen material.

Some succulents get more color in sun; others show nothing but green, no matter what degree of light they get. Most tend to change their leaf size, becoming more compact in habit and smaller in size with more sun and stress; conversely, more shading, water, and nutrients make them larger, less compact, and more lush.

1

2

3

4

5

1. Diminishing sizes of clay bowls are terraced for this collection of *Crassulaceae*. 2. This hanging 'String of Pearls' *(Senecio rowleyanus)* is more than ten years old. Here it shows its rarely seen daisylike flowers. 3. A nursery assortment showing many forms and colors of succulents. 4. *Sedum pachyphyllum* is a graceful upright. 5. This *Mammillaria pseudoperbella* is just beginning to have its crown covered with bright flowers.

1. *Echinipsis* 'Gates Hybrid'. 2. Hybrid Christmas cacti *(Schlumbergera* 'Kris Kringle' and white 'Delicata'). These are all good choices for adding color to a collection of succulents.

Guide To Selecting Succulents

The extremely diverse group called "Succulents" includes over 9,000 plants. The name (descriptive of the growth habit) applies to many different plant families, including most Cacti, all of which have the ability to withstand varying degrees of drought.

The guide on page 117 offers a partial selection. It does not list very rare succulents or those of difficult culture. If these interest you, visit one of the many specialty nurseries that carry such "collector's items."

We use botanical nomenclature to help you avoid the frustration of receiving the wrong plant when ordering or seeking additional information on a specific plant. Common names vary throughout the country, and the same name often is used for many diverse kinds of plants. Where a common name is in general usage, it appears in quotes following the botanical name.

Because succulents comprise members of so many diverse families, the following recommendations will only open the door to a world of fascinating color, form, and texture. On the list are those plants that are more generally available and of easy culture. They adapt especially well to container gardening. Some are suitable for display in floor containers; many do well in hanging baskets. Try a group of three or more that shows color contrasts as well as varied textures. The cactus groups usually found in nurseries are slow growing and will not need to graduate to larger pots for a good while.

Try the tiny *Oscularia deltoides,* with its fragrant purple-pink flowers and heady perfume, as a ground cover in a hanging basket and a potted tropical for contrast in color. (It also makes an interesting foil for a rubber plant or dumb cane.) Let your own taste and imagination be your guide— don't be timid about trying something new, as long as it is within the bounds of sound culture.

Note 1 — Any of this genus that are available in a general nursery or garden center are recommended.

Code: **DSM** = dwarf to small • **HC** = suitable for hanging container • **PT** = pot specimen for table display • **PF** = pot specimen for floor display • **SFF** = spiny but free-flowering • **FR** = fragrance • **TR** = tropical—likes acid soil, more moisture • **AR** = arid—likes slightly alkaline soil • **TR/AR** = intermediate.

A Guide to Succulents

Family	Genus	Species	Variety Or Common Name	Code
Aizoaceae	*Faucaria*	*tigrina*	Tiger's Jaw	PT-AR
		speciosa	Tiger's Jaw	PT-AR
		tuberculosa	——	PT-AR
	Fenestraria	*aurantiaca*	——	PT-AR
		rhopalophylla	Baby Toes	PT-AR
	Lithops	(Note 1)	Living Rocks	PT-AR
	Oscularia	*deltoides*	Ice Plant	HC-FR-AR
Asclepiadaceae	*Ceropegia*	*woodii*	Rosary Vine	HC-TR
			String of Hearts	HC-TR
	Hoya	*bella*	——	HC-TR-FR
		carnosa	Wax Plant	HC-TR-FR
		cultivar	'Variegata'	HC-TR-FR
		cultivar	'Exotica'	HC-TR-FR
		cultivar	'Compacta'	HC-TR-FR
	Stapelia	(Note 1)	Starfish Flower	PT-HC-TR
Cactaceae (Cacti)	*Astrophytum*	*asterias* (Note 1)	Sea Urchin Cactus	PT
	Cephalocereus	*senilis*	Old Man Cactus	PT
	Echinopsis	(Note 1)	——	SFF
		multiplex	Easter Lily Cactus	SFF
	Epiphyllum	(Note 1)	Orchid Cactus	HC-FR-TR
	Lobivia	(Note 1)	——	PT-SFF-AR
	Mammillaria	(Note 1)	——	PT-SFF-AR
	Notocactus	(Note 1)	——	PT-SFF-AR
	Rebutia	(Note 1)	——	PT-SFF-AR
	Rhipsalis	(Note 1)	Pencil Cactus	HC-TR
	Rhipsalidopsis	*gaertneri*	Easter Cactus	HC-TR
	Schlumbergera	*bridgesii*	Christmas Cactus	HC-TR
		truncata	Thanksgiving Cactus	HC-TR
Compositae (Daisy relatives)	*Senecio*	*rowleyanus*	String of Pearls	HC-TR/AR
		mikanoides	German Ivy	HC-TR/AR
Crassulaceae	*Aeonium*	*balsamiferum*	——	PT-FR-TR/AR
		arboreum	'Atroppurpureum'	PT-TR/AR
			'Schwarzkopf'	PT-TR/AR
		decorum	——	DSM-PT-TR/AR
		haworthii	Pinwheel	PT-TR/AR
		pseudotabuliforme	plain	DSM-PT-TR/AR
		pseudotabuliforme	crested	DSM-PT-TR/AR
	Crassula	*argentea*	Jade Plant	PT-PF-TR/AR
		cultivar	'Sunset'	PT-PF-TR/AR
		cooperi	——	HC-PT-DSM-TR/AR
		falcata	'Rhocea' or Scarlet Paintbrush	PT-PF-FR-TR/AR
		schmidtii	Necklace Vine	DSM-PT-TR/AR
	Echeveria	*agavoides*	——	PT-TR-/AR
		secunda	——	PT-TR/AR
		perbella	——	PT-TR/AR
	Kalanchoe	*tomentosa*	Panda Plant	PT-TR/AR
		beharensis	Felt Plant	PT-PF-TR/AR
		pumila	——	PT-HC-TR/AR
	Graptopetalum	*paraguayense*	Ghost Plant	HC-PT-TR/AR
	Sedum	*dasyphyllum*	——	DSM-HC-TR/AR
		morganianum	Burro Tail or Donkey Tail	HC-TR/AR
		multiceps	Miniature Joshua Tree (deciduous)	DSM-TR/AR
	Sempervivum	*tectorum* (Note 1)	Hen-and-Chickens	PT-TR/AR
Cycadaceae (cycads)	*Cycas*	*revoluta*	Sago Palm	PF-TR
Euphrbiaceae (Ephorbia)	*Euphorbia*	*milii*	Crown of Thorns	PT-PF-TR/AR
		caput-medusae	Medusa's Head	PT-HC-TR/AR
		obesa		PT-TR/AR
		pulcherrima	Poinsettia	PT-PF-TR/AR
Lillaceae (Lily)	*Aloe*	*aristata*	——	DSM-PT-TR/AR
		barbadensis (vera)	Medicine Plant	PT-TR/AR
	Haworthia	*fasciata*	——	PT-TR/AR
		glabrata	——	PT-TR/AR
		margaritifera	Pearl Plant	DSM-PT-TR/AR
		turgida	var. *pallidifolia*	PT-TR/AR
		setata	Lace Haworthia	DSM-PT-TR/AR
	Boweia	*volubilis* (deciduous)	Climbing Onion	DSM-PT-TR/AR
	Beaucarnea	*recurvata*	Ponytail	PT-PF-TR/AR
Oxalidaceae	*Oxalis*	*peduncularis*	——	DSM-PT-TR/AR

This *Rhododendron indicum* is 70 years old. It is in the collection at the National Arboretum.

BONSAI—NATURE IN MINIATURE

Bonsai is an ancient art form that originated in China and reached the height of its development in Japan.

The horticultural art form known as bonsai is an appreciation of nature and its many moods and settings—its towering mountains, windswept cliffs, meadows, lagoons, rushing rivers and brooks. The Japanese developed bonsai over many centuries, but today it is finding more and more devotees in the western hemisphere. The word derived originally from two Chinese symbols—"bon," meaning tray or pot, and "sai," meaning to plant; hence, "bonsai" meant container planting. But it has come to mean a very special type of container gardening—dwarfing trees to create living sculptures and reflect in miniature a segment of nature.

The general art of bonsai has its own rules for shaping, potting, and pruning. However, among the different styles that have evolved, each has its own standards for "sculpturing" and displaying, according to which kind of tree is chosen for dwarfing and which natural setting is depicted. Each bonsai, if properly shaped and potted, should look like a miniature of its mature counterpart—a tiny reproduction of nature.

These miniatures are not difficult to create, but they do make certain demands once created. Because they live in an extremely restricted space, they have special needs and require regular maintenance. If allowed to dry out, for example, they will surely die.

Bonsai for Generations

Some bonsai trees in private collections (both here and in Japan) are upwards of 350 years old. These treasures have been cherished by their owners and passed on to each succeeding generation as living heirlooms. Only a privileged few ever get to see these venerable specimens.

Some very good (and comparatively recent) collections of representative bonsai can be found in the Brooklyn Botanic Garden, the National Arboretum in Washington, D.C., the Arnold Arboretum of Massachusetts (the Larz Anderson Collection, over 50 years old), and the Huntington Botanical Garden's new collection in San Marino, California. Private collectors also exhibit some excellent specimens (a few up to 100 years old or more) in some of the major horticultural shows in the United States.

Age may have its value, but the quality of a bonsai really has to do with its appearance and the natural scene it evokes. You can begin to enjoy a bonsai of your own right away.

Because bonsai is an art imitating nature, perhaps the best way to start is to take an observational field trip. Begin to see the details of nature's art in trees—the way a trunk slants and its angle of growth as it reaches for the sun; the size of its leaves in proportion to their numbers; their shapes of leaves and their placement along the stalk (alternating, opposite); their depth of color, their texture, and the shadow pictures they draw in the changing light. Once you have begun looking at the details of trees in this way, you have truly begun the rewarding hobby of bonsai.

1

2

Above and at the top of the facing page are the five classical styles of bonsai: 1. Slanting style, with a California juniper. 2. Formal upright style, with a Japanese maple. 3. Informal upright style, with juniper. 4. Cascading style allows at least one main branch to fall below the level of the container. 5. Semi-cascading style is good for eye-level displays.

True Bonsai

As with other art forms, there are certain basic components that must be considered in their relationship to the artistic whole. The container has the same relationship to the tree as the frame does to the painting. And the container, like the frame, must never compete with the tree. Japanese bonsai containers are fine examples of restraint and simplicity. Generally, a glazed container is considered more appropriate for flowering specimens, whereas an unglazed one is chosen for foliage subjects.

To select a subject for your bonsai, first consider the trunk—this is the basis around which all other aspects of the tree will be developed.

Most Japanese bonsai are shaped from woody or semi-woody plant material. There are five classical styles of bonsai using single-trunk trees as the subject (see photos on page 121). The fundamentals of growing true bonsai or pseudobonsai appear on pages 22 and 23. Once you have selected the plant, this information will help you get started.

You can also read books on the subject (many fine ones are available), but you'll probably achieve a greater degree of early success and self-confidence by seeking out more experienced bonsai culturists. These people are usually enthusiastic about their art. They are always ready to help a beginner and to share their knowledge. The International Bonsai Society is growing in the U.S. To obtain the address of the Akebono Bonsai Society or study group in your area, write to: Ben T. Suzuki, Nippon Bonsai Association, 608 N. 21st Street, Montebello, California 90640. Or you may write to the American Bonsai Society, 1363 W. Sixth Street, Erie, Pennsylvania 16505.

3

4

5

Below: The Japanese black pine *(Pinus thunbergiana)*.

How to Get Started with Bonsai

Containers for bonsai come in many sizes and shapes. Some are glazed, others are not. Colors tend toward white and brown, with some subtle tones of sand and rock. The form of the subject to be planted dictates the choice of the pot.

You will need a few tools. Most nurseries and garden centers carry basic supplies, including wire cutters, pruning shears, and annealed copper wire (best for bonsai). The wire should be just slightly more rigid than the branches to be trained. You'll also need two or three sizes of dull-pointed sticks (like chopsticks) for removing soil from roots and untangling twisted roots.

Nursery stock offers the most available source of plants from which to start your first bonsai. Often, nurseries discard plants with dwarfed trunks or irregular branching, but this is just the sort of thing you're looking for. Discards usually are much cheaper, which adds to their appeal as good subjects for your first bonsai project.

A commercial nursery's procedure. We took our photographer to a wholesale nursery that specializes in commercial bonsai production—Select-Nurseries, Inc. in Brea, California. The photos and text that follow illustrate the steps they use in creating bonsai. You can follow the same procedures if you buy a tree in a gallon can at your nursery. A word of caution, however: *Don't work in the sun or wind—* roots dry out fast.

Step 1. Examine your subject, viewing it from all sides. Decide which should be the "front" side.

Step 2. Remove the tree from the container, holding the trunk firmly at the base. Use a long knife or spatula to loosen the rootball from the sides. Tap gently and patiently to loosen from the bottom.

Step 3. Begin at the base of the tree and prune unwanted branches and stems. Eliminate *opposite* branching. Strive for *alternate* branches and alternate stems on the branches for an asymmetric form. Remove growth from the *underside* of the branches.

Prune so that light will strike all branches equally. Proper pruning helps bring good ventilation to all areas of your tree.

Step 4. You must wire branches in order to shape them. (A visit to a nursery or garden center where bonsai is displayed will show you how plants are shaped and how wire is used.)

It helps to practice the wiring technique on some scrap branches so that you get the feeling of bending a branch and noting its flexibility or rigidity.

To wire your bonsai, measure off lengths of wire equal to the length of the branch(es) plus at least one-third more.

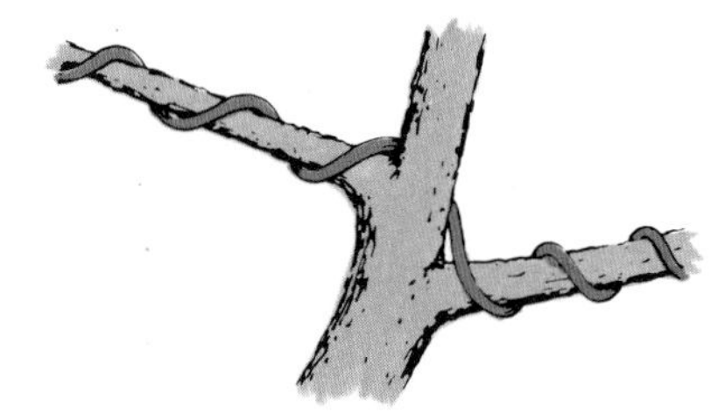

One wire may hold two branches if they are close on the trunk. Wrap the wire clockwise on one side, counterclockwise on the other side. This prevents the wire from girdling the trunk as the plant grows.

Anchor the wire at the base of a single branch by overlapping it.

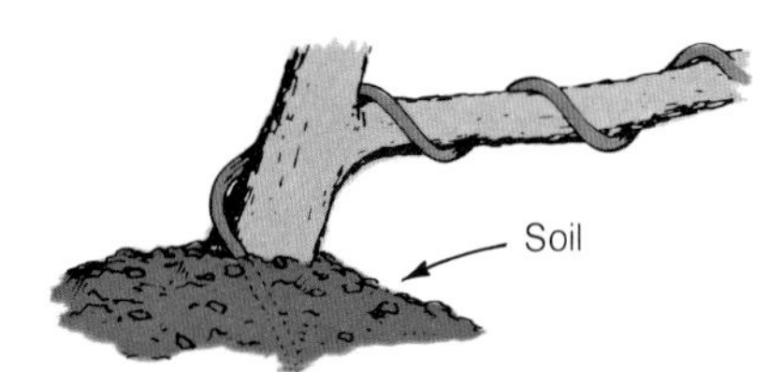

Near the base of the plant, the wire may be anchored in the soil.

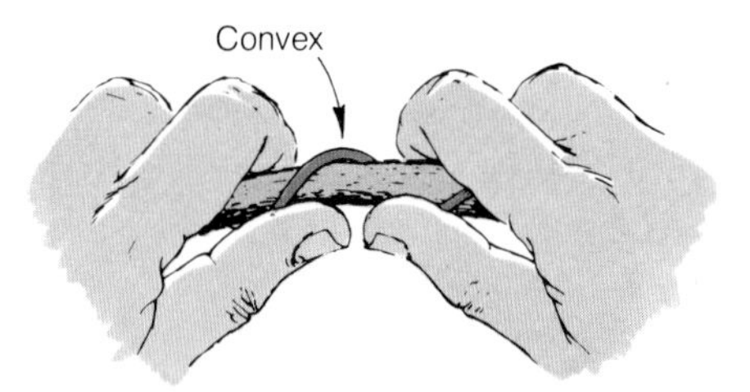

When bending a branch, be sure that your thumbs brace *under* the curve where the wire wraps convexly, or else you may snap the branch and ruin the form of the tree.

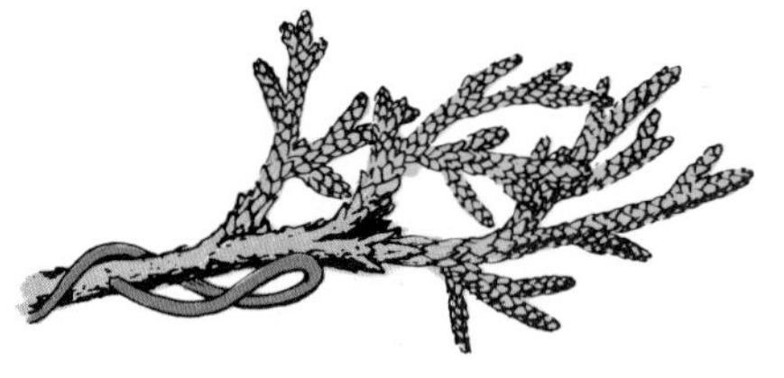

When you reach the tip of the branch with the wiring, snip off any excess wire and bend it backward and close-in to the stem of the branch.

Don't wrap too tightly. Branches must have growing room. Wire is not applied to restrict growth, only to shape. Wires that bite into bark make ugly marks that last for years.

Step 5. To prepare the tree for its new container, you'll need the following equipment: a pruning shears; dull-pointed sticks (like chopsticks); a pail of water to which you've added a few drops of a chemical "starter solution"; potting mix and a bonsai container with window screen mesh to cover drainage holes.

First, the rootball must be greatly reduced. If it's currently a tangled mass of roots, use the chopstick to remove soil and untangle the snarl of roots girdling the ball. Don't damage new feeder roots (the small, light-colored ones). Older roots are thicker, often wiry, and usually much darker. *Roots should spread in all four directions evenly.* Prune a third of all the long, older roots you untangled.

Keep feeder roots moist by dipping them frequently into the pail of water. Work quickly but carefully.

When you've removed a third of the total rootball, put a thick layer of potting mix in the bottom of the container, and place the tree in that. If the container has an oval or oblong shape, place the tree off-center about two-thirds the distance from the edge, allowing the longest branch to spread directly above the surface area and the shorter branch to spread directly over the other third. A square or round container usually calls for a center placement.

Holding the tree with one hand, settle the rootball into the soil; use a stick to spread the roots around the base evenly.

Sprinkle more soil over the roots, covering them. Press the soil down to fill in all spaces between roots. Firm the spot around them.

If a stubborn root won't stay down, bend a short length of wire into a hairpin shape, then place it over the root and firm it into the soil to hold the root in place. You can remove this later, once the root has established itself in the soil.

Next, set the container in water until the top of the soil is moist. Add a top dressing, such as moss or pebbles.

Now is the time to make any changes in the direction of your branches by bending them carefully. Think of yourself as a sculptor.

Display your finished sc[...] tered, not direct, sun. Mist th[...] maintain your bonsai, don't a[...] out. Also, pinch off new, unwa[...] before it becomes woody. This the need for heavy pruning.

Pseudo-Bonsai

This method is for the imaginative and creative gardener who hasn't the time to devote to true bonsai, or who would rather go for the instant effect of pseudo-bonsai before plunging into the more painstaking horticultural processes involved in the art of true bonsai.

To get a bonsai "feeling," the gardener/artist creates a pleasing esthetic relationship of container to plant. Which plants to choose and how to shape or "sculpt" the material used depends on your creativity and personal taste. Pseudo-bonsai is free of the classical Japanese rules, but you will probably get better results if you keep them in mind—they relate to the total effect. Your plant material can be as unlikely and untraditional as you wish—you can use a seedling plant or even a root-bound plant.

You might even choose a succulent. The jade plant is easy, or try an ice plant, an oxalis, a geranium, or a coleus.

When using such material as succulents and coleus, you are not actually dwarfing a plant in this instant bonsai procedure; you are merely creating a mood.

Eventually your plant will need to be repotted. Probably it also will require frequent but easy pruning to maintain its bonsai feeling. Some of the succulent material will not require repotting so much as pinching off new growth as it appears. Other plants, like the coleus, may outgrow their bonsai life. If so, make cuttings and start again with a fresh plant to create another bonsai mood.

Pseudo-bonsai, of course, requires good horticultural practices—watering and feeding, according to the kind of plant you are growing.

A container well suited to its purpose. The trellis supports the vine, and moveable shelves support the melons.

CONTAINERS TO MAKE

You can make containers and create growing surfaces to accommodate even the most restricted spaces.

The pages that follow show plans and photographs of some homemade and custom-built wooden containers.

Many container gardeners prefer to be given merely the plan of a box or a tub, rather than specific directions. It can be more challenging that way—directions are meant to be followed, but a plan can always be improved upon. That's why there are about as many containers as there are container gardeners.

Redwood and cedar are the best kinds of wood to use. They are relatively rot-resistant, and they weather attractively without paint or stain. Redwood should be heart grade (no sap wood) and both types of wood should be air or kiln dried.

Although exterior plywood is specified for the bottom of the containers, redwood or cedar boards are equally satisfactory. Plywood edges must be sealed (see page 36).

You can provide adequate drainage with ½-inch holes spaced 5 inches apart. When using a lightweight, fine soil mix, cover the holes with a fine mesh screen such as aluminum fly screen.

The Vertical Dimension

If your floor space is too limited to accommodate all the plants you want to grow, try using the vertical dimension.

To the container gardener, every smooth vertical surface is a potential gardening area. A 6-foot-high, 20-foot-long fence will add a surprising 120 square feet to a small garden.

Although some gardening experts claim that "vine crops such as melons, cucumbers, squash, and others that require considerable space may not be advisable in the small garden," the small-space gardener assumes that any wide-spreading vine can be trained to grow up instead of out.

A vertical vine won't, by itself, support heavy fruits such as melon and squash, but a few short shelves built onto the fence to take the weight of the crop will also take the weight off the vines.

If you already have a fence on your property, use it to display wooden planter boxes of various dimensions. If you use brackets or shelves to support the planters, you can change your live show as often as you want. Square-sided wire half-baskets can be used against a fence or walk to hold sphagnum moss.

Checkerboard fence. There are also other ways in which small-space gardeners can use a fence. By slightly altering the construction of a fence panel, you can turn it into a checkerboard planter and display area. Use 4″ × 6″ posts in the section you wish to plant. Cover the back of the fence with regular fencing material (1″ × 6″ or 1″ × 8″ boards). Use 2″ × 6″s for the verticals and cross pieces between the posts. You also can use 4″ × 4″ posts and a girdle of 2″ × 4″s, but the width of the 2″ × 4″s is too shallow to maintain easily.

In the planting area itself, staple wire mesh (a welded wire with a 2″ × 2″ or 2″ × 2½″ mesh is ideal). Cover the edges of wire with wood facing strips. Work in a

Two versions of the checkerboard fence.

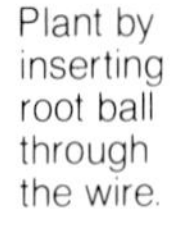

Plant by inserting root ball through the wire.

½- to 1-inch-thick layer of sphagnum moss, starting from the bottom of the wire. For the moment, leave open space at the top of the wire; then fill the wire up to the top with lightweight planter mix. Put straight sphagnum moss on top of the mix.

Free-standing vertical wall. A space-hungry gardener, realizing how successful a vertical planting scheme can be, may want to use the entire fence as a planting area. This is possible—indeed, the vertical garden wall is popular in Europe—but it calls for a specialized construction. Inside wire braces are needed to keep large areas of wire mesh from bulging with the weight of the plantings. Installing one or two wire-mesh partitions in a 6-foot-high wall will keep the filler mix from settling too much.

Instead of wire and sphagnum moss, you also can use black plastic film to build a simplified European planter. To make a free-standing box that is 8 inches wide, 34 inches long, 44 inches deep, and meant to front a hedge 8 feet high, cut end pieces of 2″ × 8″ rough redwood 6 feet long. These form the posts, which are inserted in the ground when the box is complete. Cross brace the ends with 2″ × 2″s at the top and bottom. Use exterior plywood for the back and bottom, drilling drainage holes in the bottom piece. Secure the black plastic film for the front of the box with a grid of 1″ × 2″s on 6-inch centers. These hold the plastic and the planter mix behind it.

When inserting plants, work in some damp sphagnum moss to plug the hole in the plastic.

This roll-around box is planted with lettuce in early spring. In the summer the lettuce could be replaced with your favorite annuals.

Roll-around wall. You can plant the free-standing vertical box on both sides. If you do, however, widen the box to at least 10 inches. Attach some wheels to the planter so that it can be moved about to get all the sun or part shade it requires. In spring, you can have lettuce on one side and pansies on the other. Through summer, with the roll-around parked on a shady patio, you can have impatiens in the front and back.

To water the soil mix evenly, place vertical 1¼-inch plastic pipes 6 inches apart in the box, as you add the soil. Cap the sections of pipe at the bottom, and drill holes for even watering.

You also can riddle the pipe with ¼-inch holes. Then, you can water the top of the wall to take care of the first 2 feet of soil and use the pipes to water the lower 2 feet. However, if you are using only pipes for watering, follow these instructions:

1. Drill no holes below 1 foot from the bottom, except for a 1/16-inch hole in the cap to let the pipe drain slowly.
2. Drill six holes ⅛ inch in diameter, 2 feet from the bottom.
3. Drill six holes 3/16 inch in diameter, 3 feet from the bottom.
4. Drill six holes ¼ inch in diameter in the top foot. This graduation in hole size is to compensate for the difference in water "head" between the top and bottom when you first fill the pipe.

This petunia "tree" was made with a half circle of 2" mesh wire, stapled to a 1" × 12" board. A lining of sphagnum moss retains the planter mix. Petunia seedlings were inserted through the moss.

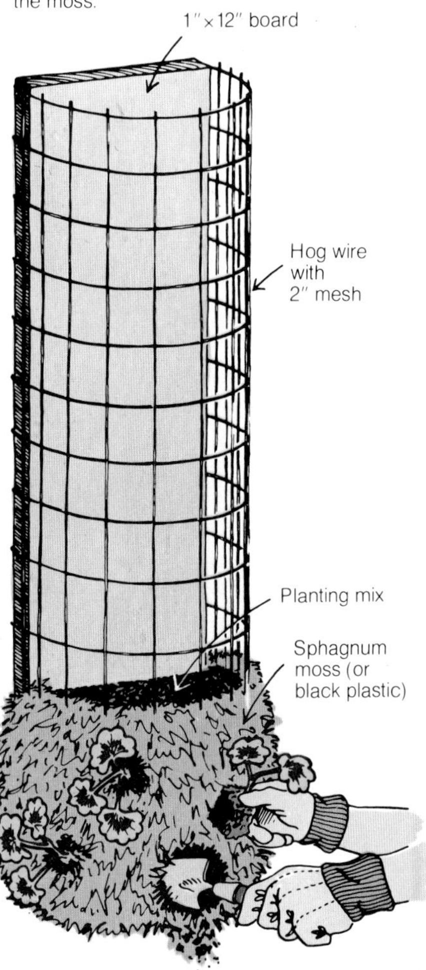

To line the wire with plastic (see text for detailed instructions):

Pillars of flowers. If you like the idea of vertical planting but consider a wall garden or roll-around too complex, you can make a flowering pillar instead. You'll need a piece of 1" × 6" redwood or cedar cut to the desired length, and welded wire with a 2" × 2" or 2" × 2½" mesh. A 14-inch wide length of wire will form a half circle when bent and stapled to the board. Use exterior-grade plywood cut in a half circle as a base for the pillar; the dimensions should be the same as for the half circle of wire. Staple or nail the wire's edges to the back edge of the board and plywood base. Work ½ inch of damp sphagnum moss into the wire. The pillar can be 4 feet, 8 feet, or anything in between. Fill the column with dampened, lightweight planter mix. Plant as you would a hanging wire basket (see page 40). When securing the pillar to a wall, protect the wall with a backing of roofing paper fastened to the backboard of the pillar.

You also can use black plastic film instead of sphagnum moss to contain the planter mix. To keep the plastic neat and wrinkle-free, cut it about 2 inches longer than the wire and 2 to 3 inches wider. Fold the extra 2 inches of plastic over the top of the wire. Staple the wire and plastic to one side of the board. Bend the wire in a half circle, guiding the overlapped plastic as you bend the wire. Make sure that the plastic is smooth and straight against the wire; then staple the wire and plastic to the other side of the board.

When filling the column with the mix, lean it forward so that the mix falls against the plastic.

Using a 12-inch-wide backboard, you can make pillars either with wire and sphagnum moss or with plastic. In the wire pillar, you can put strawberries and fibrous begonias. In the plastic-lined pillar, you can plant 'Small Fry' tomatoes both at the top and halfway down.

Popular flowers for pillars are pansies, violas, or a combination of alyssum and violas. You might also try impatiens, fibrous begonias, and petunias.

Precautions: Before applying the sphagnum moss, loosen and moisten it evenly.

Before you add the planter mix, water it; then, once it's damp, pour it into the containers. The mix will settle after the first watering. Then add more mix (dampened as before).

Watermelon Box

This box with adjustable trellis is designed to provide adequate support for vines and fruit of watermelons but may be used for other vine crops such as squash or cantaloupes. Movable shelves support the fruit and may be placed wherever the plant decides to produce it.

If you check the drawing you will see that the sides and ends of the container can be assembled as units before being attached to each other. Be careful when placing the bottom cleats (C) and the vertical ones (F). The former are raised enough to allow room for the bottom; the others are situated so the container sides will be flush with the ends. Remember that the pieces designated as (A) are 2 inches longer than the other side pieces so they act as legs to elevate the box above grade. You can substitute screws for nails if you wish, but in either case it's a good idea to coat all mating surfaces with waterproof glue. Cut the bottom to fit *after* the container parts have been assembled. Drill drain holes.

Cut all parts for the trellis to the lengths called out in the materials list. Do the assembly by attaching the top strip to the sides, then add the horizontal pieces and finally the vertical ones.

The carriage bolt and wing nut are used so the trellis can be pivoted to a desirable position. The trellis can be supported by wall or fence. If not, cut suitable length of ¾- by 1½-inch stock that you can use as a prop.

Make two or three movable shelves to start. Hopefully, you'll need more.

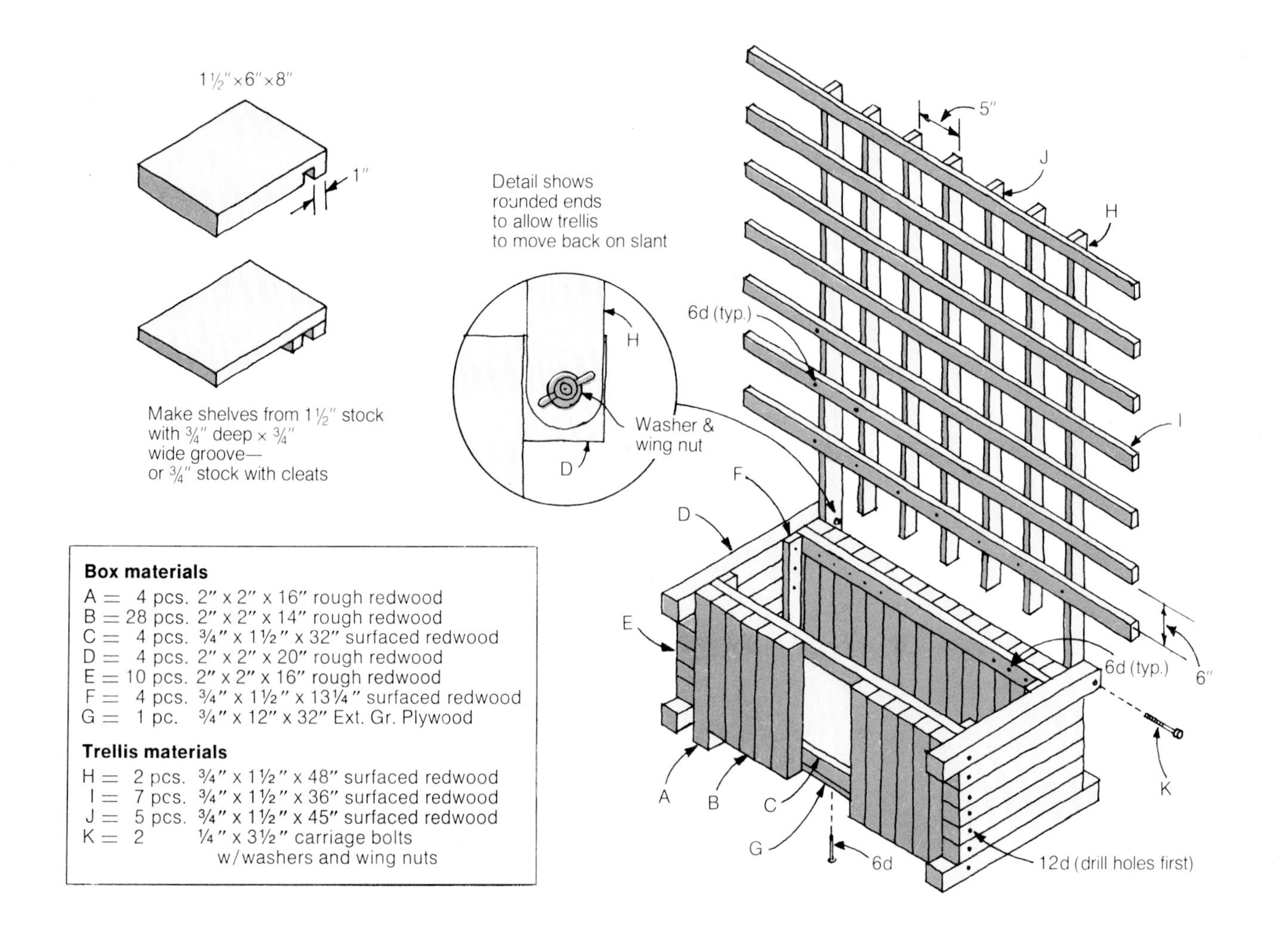

The rootballs of plants to be inserted through the sphagnum moss need to be moist, not wet. Therefore, water the 6-pack or flat about 3 hours before removing the plants.

Unless you've mixed a timed-release fertilizer into the planter mix, apply diluted liquid fertilizer every third or fourth watering.

Water to moisten the mix from top to bottom. Keep watering until you can see water dripping from the drainage holes at the bottom.

Don't underestimate the weight of these large planters. Dry, the soil mix may be lightweight, but it holds a lot of water, and water weighs 8.3 pounds per gallon.

A-Frame Trellis

The A-frame trellis may be used with two containers or as a freestanding unit to support vine plants sowed directly in the ground. The hinge arrangement at the top provides for span and height adjustments so you have considerable leeway when spacing containers or seed rows. To stir your imagination, consider that the project, when not used as an "A," may be opened completely and braced vertically to provide a trellis 4½" high by 12" long.

Cut all parts for the trellis to correct length. Do the assembly by nailing the legs (6-foot pieces) to all the horizontal strips and then adding the verticals. Cut one piece of material 6 inches long and use it as a gauge for correct spacing. The 4d nails called for are adequate but if you want more strength use 6d nails and clinch them on the back. Use 2-inch brass hinges with brass screws. Place one at each end and a third one in the center.

The containers shown are butt-jointed with glue and 7d nails. Add the bottom by nailing from the outside. The feet are 4-inch lengths cut from 4- × 4-inch stock, secured with glue and nails driven from the inside of the container. The cap strips are optional but add enough to the appearance of the project to make the addition worthwhile.

Don't neglect to provide drain holes.

The trellis is a separate unit. It can be used with various containers or even for ground plantings.

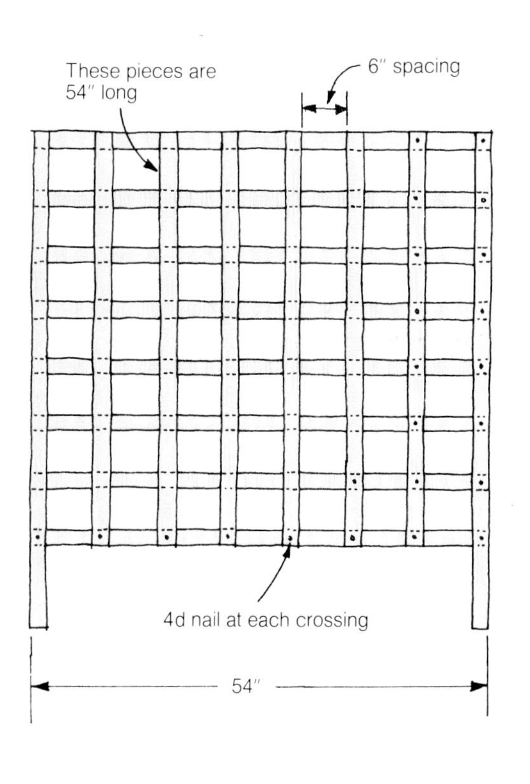

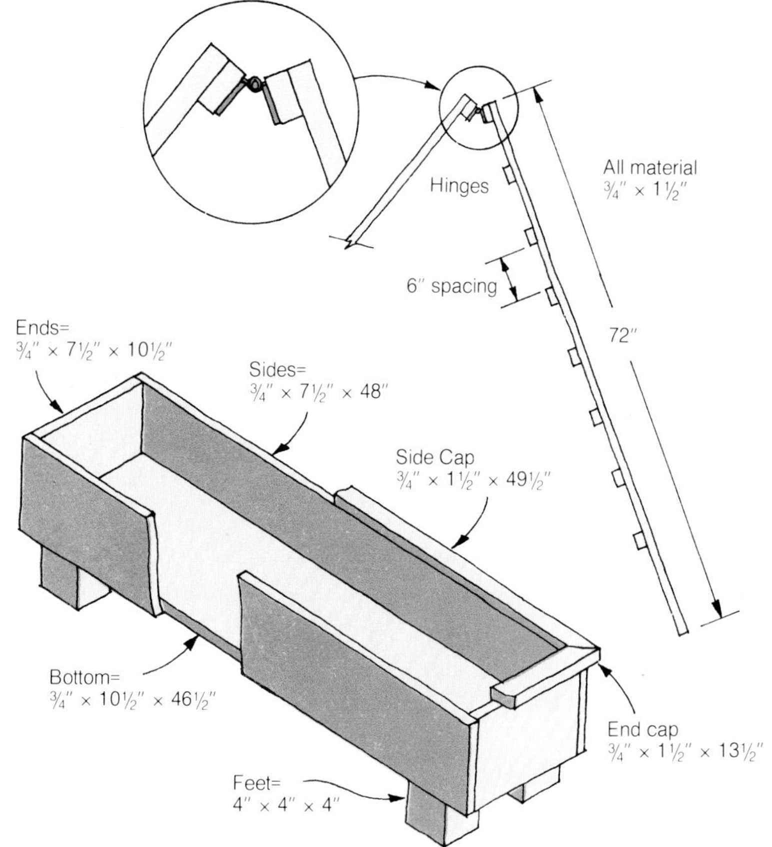

Simple is frequently also elegant.

Step by Step to a Simple Box

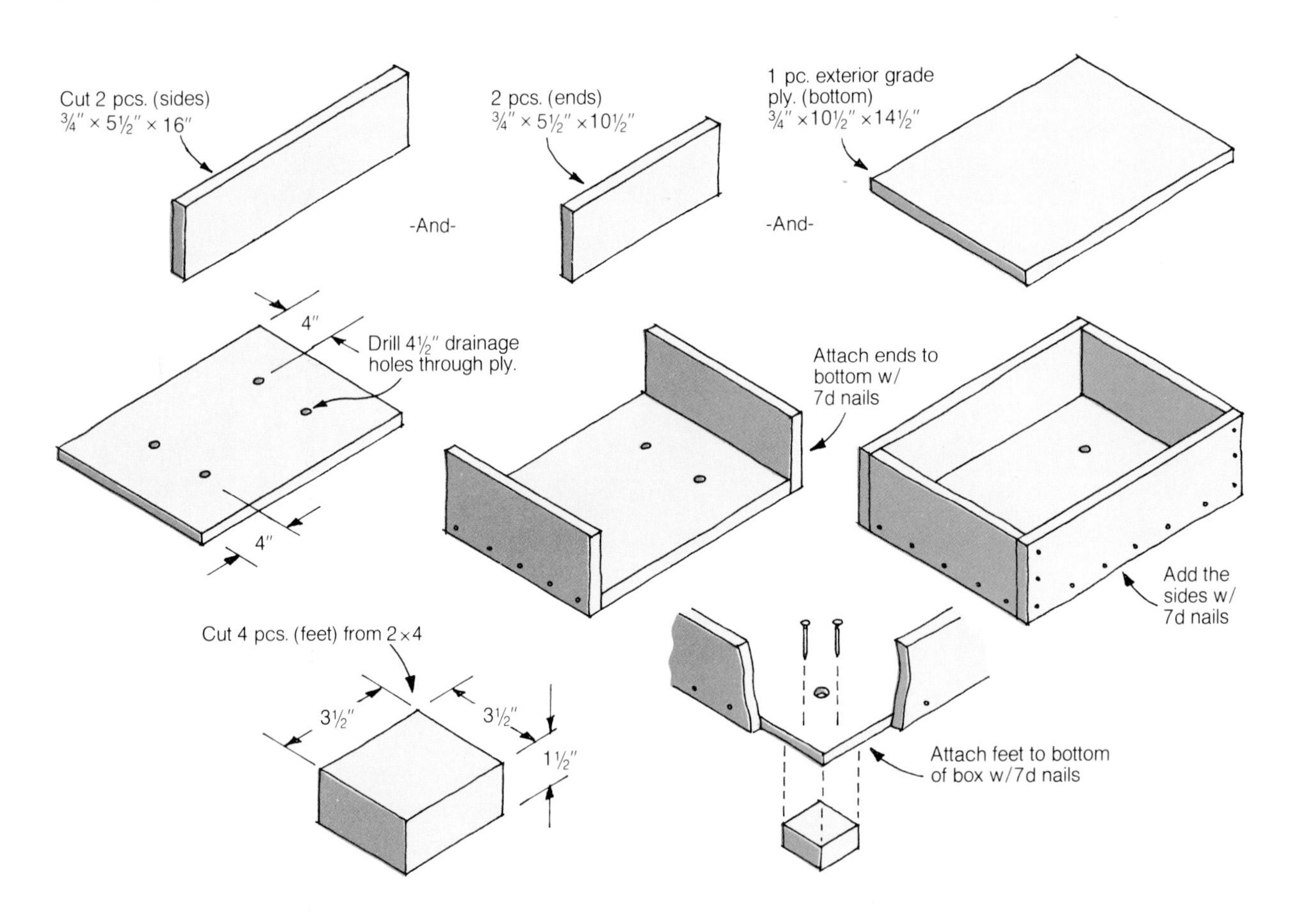

Cut 2 pcs. (sides)
¾" × 5½" × 16"
-And-
2 pcs. (ends)
¾" × 5½" × 10½"
-And-
1 pc. exterior grade
ply. (bottom)
¾" × 10½" × 14½"
4"
Drill 4½" drainage
holes through ply.
4"
Attach ends to
bottom w/
7d nails
Add the
sides w/
7d nails
Cut 4 pcs. (feet) from 2×4
3½"
3½"
1½"
Attach feet to bottom
of box w/7d nails

Various combinations and modular displays are possible by using the wooden sleeves and reversible bases.

Multipurpose Box

If you bring home a dozen 'Petite' marigolds, the 3-inch-deep box will show off the 8-inch-high plants better than a deep box.

But, if the marigolds are the variety 'Hawaii', better use the 6-inch-deep box.

This box starts with a 6-inch depth and varies in height in multiples of 2 and 4 inches. Your box might be any combination of depths.

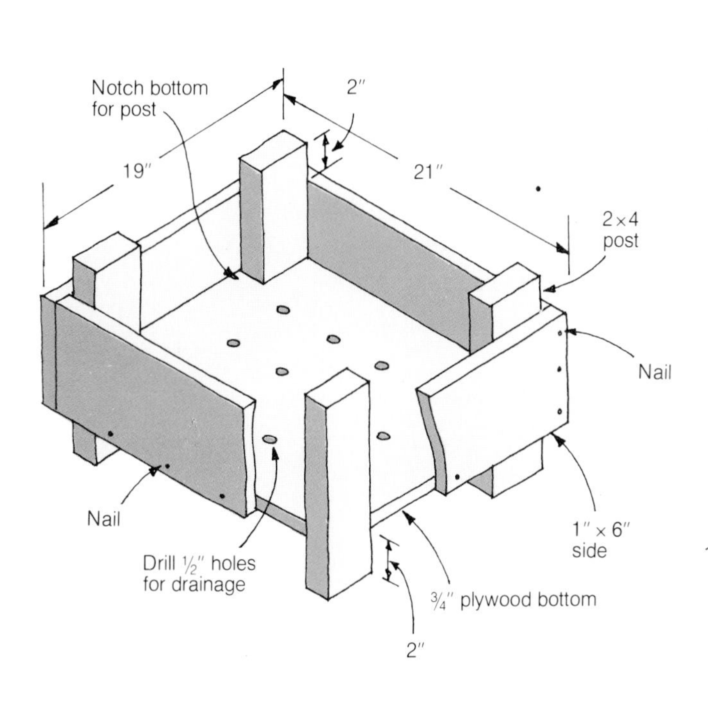

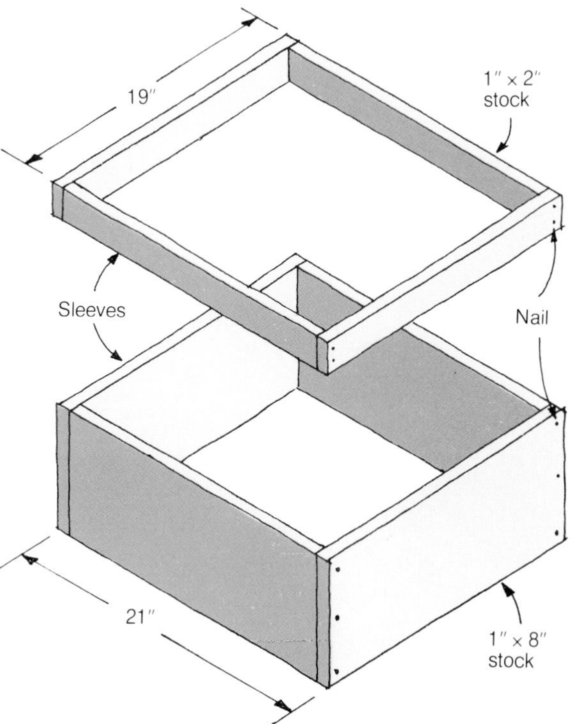

There are 6- and 7-inch pots in this display.

A single box holds a tomato plant in a 5-gallon can.

Our multipurpose box is dimensioned to suit the container and pot sizes shown at the right. The project consists of an invertible base, plus two sleeves which slip over the projecting corner posts. Either sleeve may be used regardless of the base position. For example, use the base bottom-down and with the large sleeve, for a 5-gallon can, or with the bottom up and the small sleeve, for low pots.

Attach the ends of the base to the corner posts and then add the sides. Size the bottom to fit and then cut the notches for the corner posts.

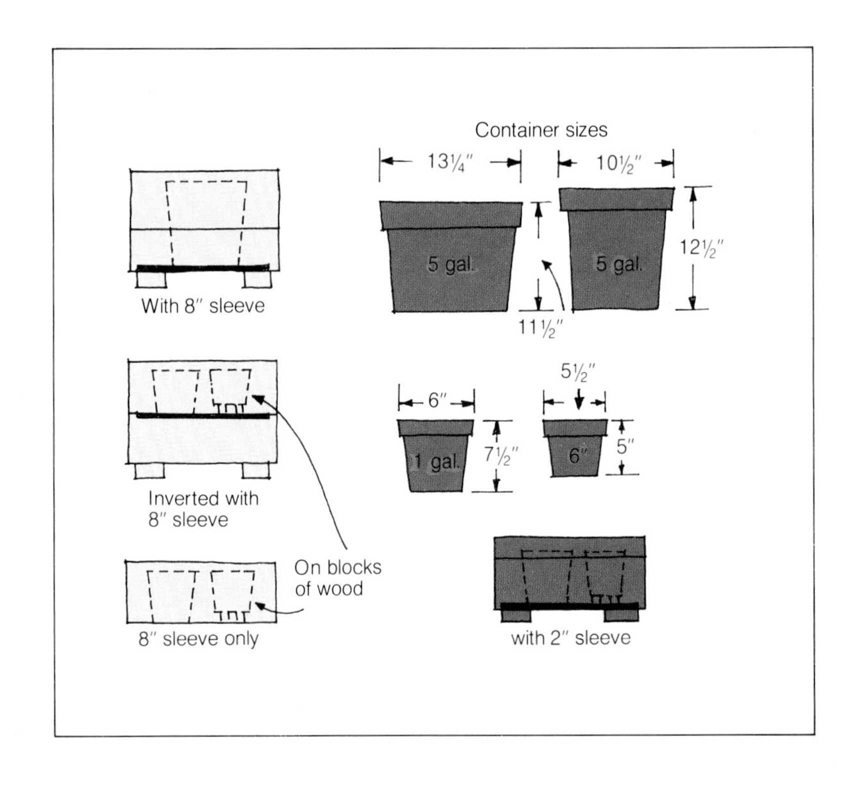

A single box with 6-inch pots of begonias resting on a reversible base.

Top views with 5 gal., 1 gal., and 6″ containers

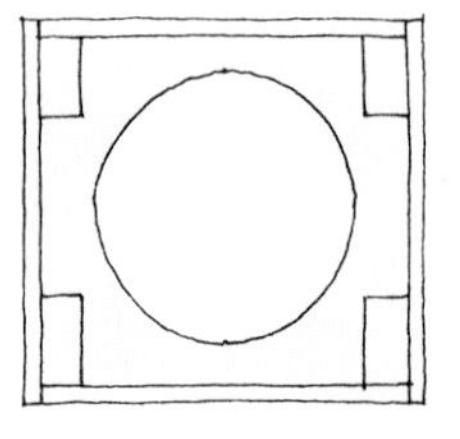

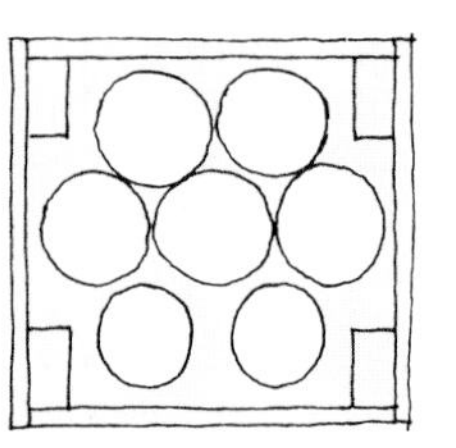

Tub Planter

This planter is easier to make than it looks. However, you do need a table saw with blade-angle adjustment and dado attachments.

½″ ¼″ ⅝″ ½″ ⅜″ 8″ & 11″ 3″ 1″ 9″

Cut and dado staves to match this drawing. Be sure to use "rough cut" lumber so it's a full 1″ thick—if it isn't, you'll have to revise the bottom diameter.

Hold the staves together in two or three groups with galvanized staples in the bottom.

Put these groups around the bottom and hold them all together with the banding material.

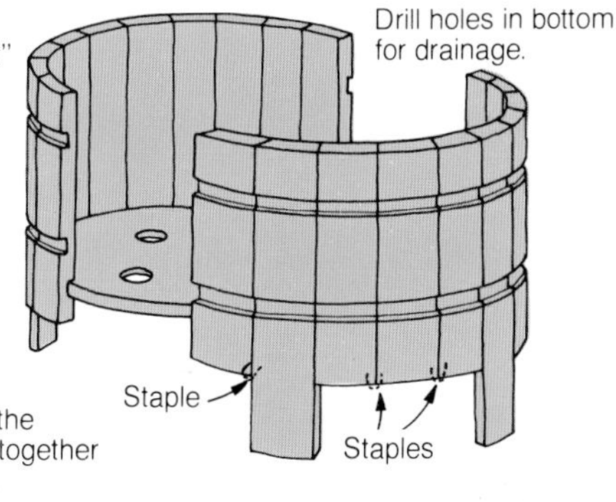

Staple

Metal or plastic strapping can be tacked to one stave, pulled tight around the others with pliers, and tacked again.

Wire or metal clotheslines can be wrapped around two or three times and the ends stapled.

Plastic clothesline can be cinched tight by putting a loop at one end, running the other end around the staves through the loop (see drawing), and pulling back hard. Staple or tack the end.

Materials Needed:

Rough redwood—
15 staves: 1″ × 3″ × 8¼″
5 staves: 1″ × 3″ × 11″

Exterior plywood—
1 bottom: ½″ × 18″ diameter

Miscellaneous—
Galvanized staples
Banding (see construction notes)

Scrap or Stick Planters

Straight-cut Octagon

Cut a circle for bottom and drill drain holes.

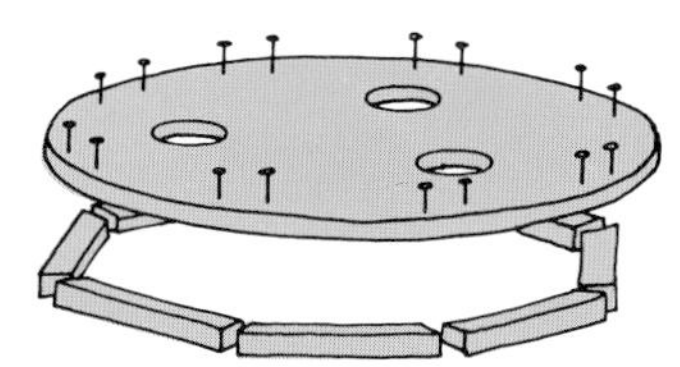

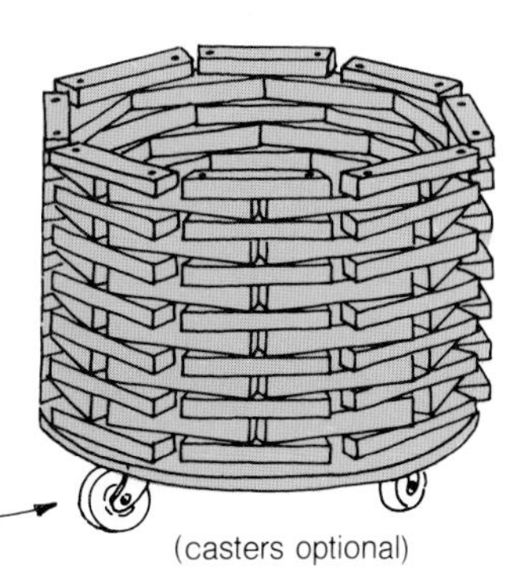

(casters optional)

Arrange eight of the 5″ pieces in a regular octagon. Lay the bottom on top of them and nail it to them.

Turn the bottom, with its tier of 5″ pieces attached, right side up and nail on the second tier. Add the third and successive tiers in the same manner.

If you wish to miter the corners as shown for the hexagon planter, angle the cut at 22.5°.

Mitered Hexagon

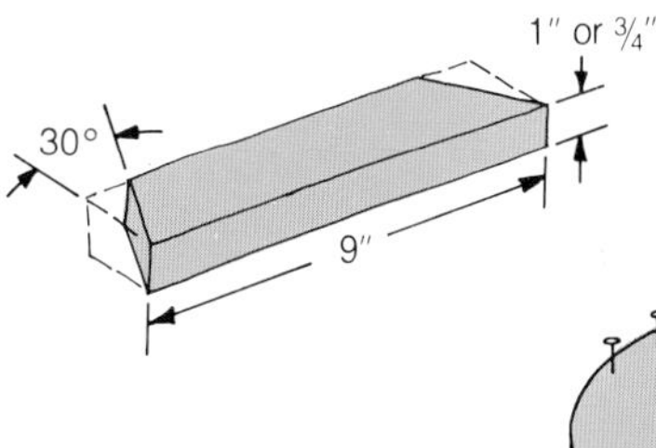

The 30° mitered ends let the pieces fit snugly, for a more tailored appearance.

As with the octagon, start by laying the first tier on the floor and nailing on the bottom. Turn it over and nail on each successive tier.

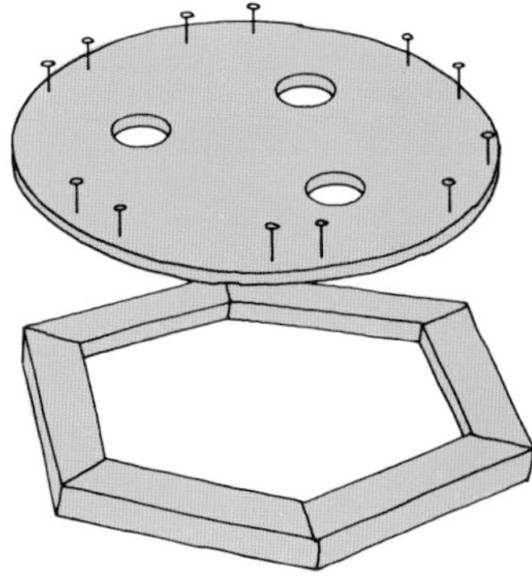

Create different looks by varying the relationship of the tiers.

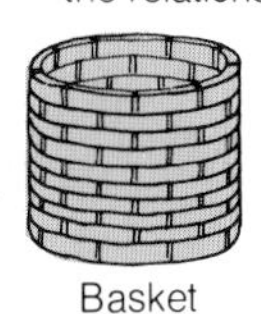

Basket

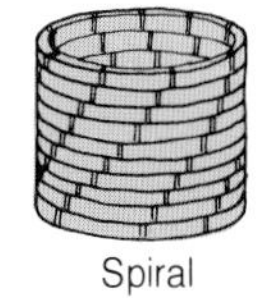

Spiral

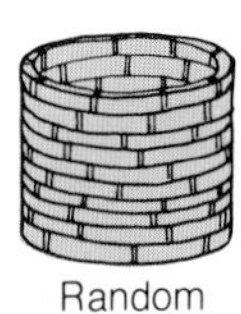

Random

Materials Needed:

Straight-cut octagon:

Scrap wood—
Sides: 104 pieces 1″×2″×5″
Bottom: 2 pieces 1″×8″×15″
or 1 piece ½″ plywood 15″ dia.

Miscellaneous—
Galvanized box nails (many)
3 or 4 casters (optional)

Mitered hexagon:

Scrap wood—
Sides: 98 pieces 1″ × 2″ × 9″
with 30° miter on each end

Bottom: 2 pieces 1″×8″×15″
or 1 piece ½″ plywood 15″ dia.

Miscellaneous—
Galvanized box nails
3 or 4 casters (optional)

Grandpa Fabri's Planter

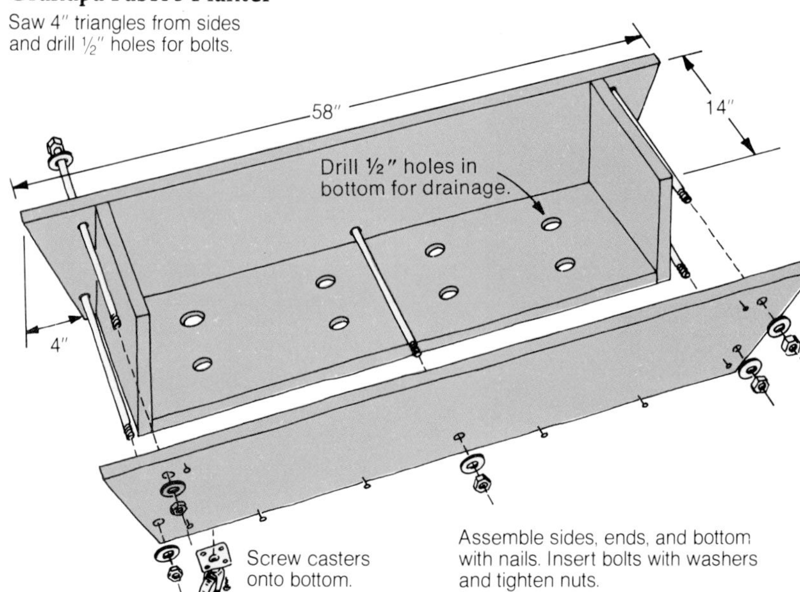

Saw 4" triangles from sides and drill ½" holes for bolts.
58"
14"
Drill ½" holes in bottom for drainage.
4"
Screw casters onto bottom.
Assemble sides, ends, and bottom with nails. Insert bolts with washers and tighten nuts.

Materials Needed:

Rough redwood—
2 sides: 1"×12"× 58"
2 ends: 1"×12"×14"
Exterior plywood—
1 bottom: ¾"×14"× 48"

Miscellaneous—
5 bolts: ½"×18"
with washers and nuts
Galvanized box nails
4 heavy-duty casters

Carpenter's Tool-box Planter

This attractive planter moves easily from place to place and may be converted into a mini greenhouse.

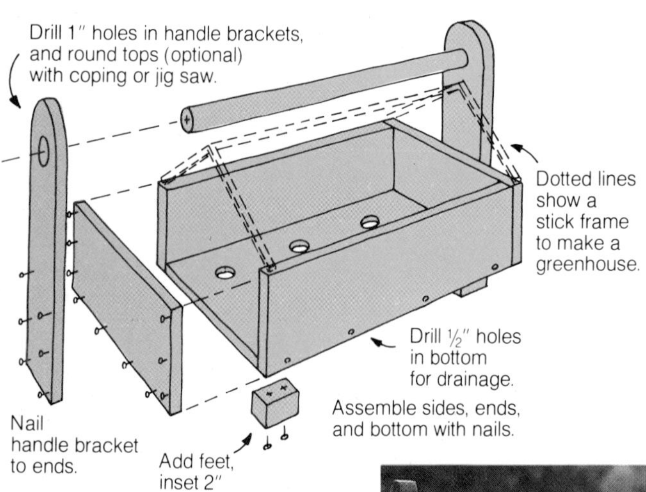

Drill 1" holes in handle brackets, and round tops (optional) with coping or jig saw.
Dotted lines show a stick frame to make a greenhouse.
Drill ½" holes in bottom for drainage.
Assemble sides, ends, and bottom with nails.
Nail handle bracket to ends.
Add feet, inset 2" from edges.

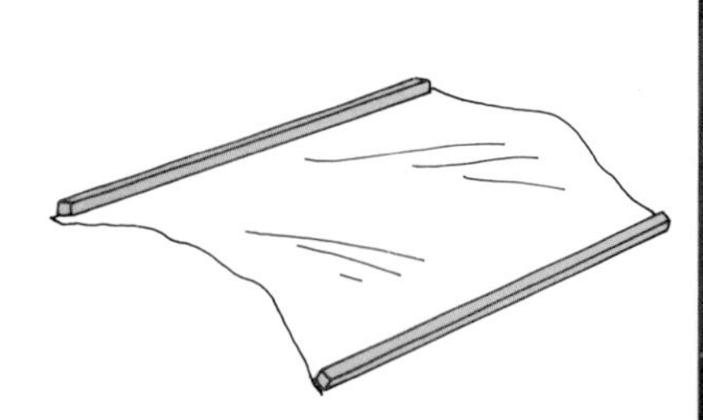

To make a greenhouse, add the stick frame shown on the drawing. Tack 21" sticks to a square of clear plastic and lay the combination over the frame. One side may be flopped over the handle to provide ventilation.

Materials Needed:

Finished redwood—
2 sides: 1" × 6" × 20"
2 ends: 1" × 6" × 14"
2 handle brackets
1" × 4" × 17½"
4 feet: 2" × 2" × 3"

Miscellaneous—
1 handle: 1" hardwood dowel, 24" long
Galvanized box nails

Additional materials needed for seed starting—
4 sticks: ½" × ½" × 10"
2 sticks: ½" × ½" × 21"
1 stick: ½" × ½" × 22"
Clear plastic film: 22" × 22"

Assemble box sides, ends, and bottom with nails or screws.

24″ 16″ 6″

For outdoor use, drill drain holes in bottom.

Whittle corners from about 6″ of handle with plane or knife.

12″ 24″ 9″

Assemble frame with bolts, screws, or nails.

Fasten wheel pieces together with cross braces. Drill 2″ hole in center. Cut wheel circle with coping or jig saw.

Attach wheel to frame with pipe straps and screws.

Put axle through wheel. Drill $\frac{1}{8}$″ holes in axle on each side of wheel. Slip on washers and insert cotter pins.

Wheelbarrow Planter

Materials Needed:

Rough redwood—
Wheel: 3 pieces 2″ × 4″ × 12″
4 pieces $\frac{1}{2}$″ × 2″ × 8″
Box: 2 pieces 1″ × 6″ × 24″
2 pieces 1″ × 6″ × 16″
Frame: 2 pieces 2″ × 2″ × 54″
1 piece 2″ × 2″ × 13″
2 pieces 2″ × 2″ × 17″
Exterior plywood—
1 bottom: $\frac{3}{4}$″ × 16″ × 22″

Miscellaneous—
Axle: Dowel, 2″×10″
or pipe, 2″×10″
2 washers, 2″ I.D.
2 large cotter pins
2 pipe straps, 2″
Galvanized box nails
Galvanized nuts and bolts (optional)
Galvanized wood screws (optional)

John Mathias Planters

Wood-Base Planter

Nail (or bolt) joist hangers to sides, 20″ apart. Attach ends to these hangers.

Paint all metal parts before assembling.

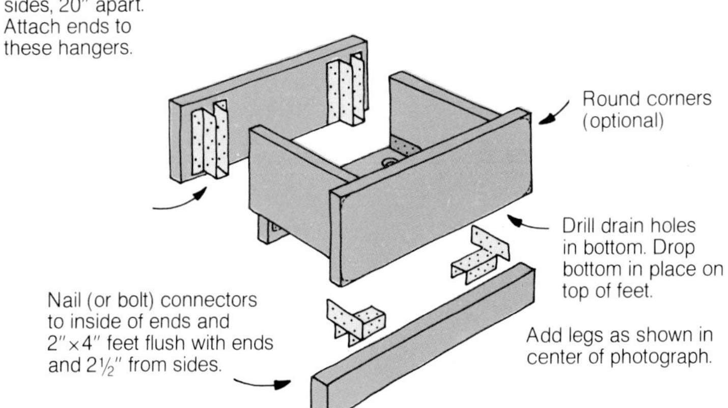

Round corners (optional)

Drill drain holes in bottom. Drop bottom in place on top of feet.

Nail (or bolt) connectors to inside of ends and 2″×4″ feet flush with ends and 2$\frac{1}{2}$″ from sides.

Add legs as shown in center of photograph.

Metal-legged Planter

Metal post anchor.

Attach filler blocks to sides, then post anchors to blocks and sides.

Set ends in place on metal seats on post anchors. Nail to filler blocks.

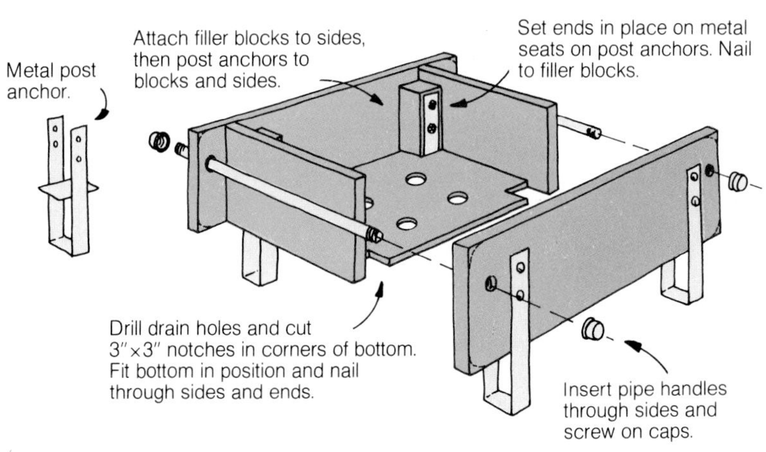

Drill drain holes and cut 3″×3″ notches in corners of bottom. Fit bottom in position and nail through sides and ends.

Insert pipe handles through sides and screw on caps.

Materials Needed:

For Wood-Base Planter:

Finished redwood—
2 sides: 2″×12″×28″
2 ends: 2″×12″×20″
2 feet: 2″×4″×23$\frac{1}{2}$″

Exterior plywood—
1 bottom: $\frac{1}{2}$″×20″×20″

Connectors—
4 joist hangers, 1$\frac{5}{8}$″×10$\frac{1}{2}$″
4 metal connectors

Miscellaneous—
Metal paint
Galvanized box nails
24 bolts, $\frac{1}{8}$″×$\frac{1}{4}$″ (optional)

For Metal-Legged Planter:

Finished redwood—
2 sides: 1″×12″×28″
2 ends: 1″×12″×14″
4 blocks: 3″×3″×9″

Exterior plywood—
1 bottom: $\frac{1}{2}$″×14″×24″

Connectors—
4 post anchors, 4″×4″

Miscellaneous—
8 bolts, $\frac{3}{8}$″×4$\frac{1}{2}$″, with nuts and washers
2 pieces of pipe, $\frac{1}{2}$″×18″
4 pipe caps, $\frac{1}{2}$″
Galvanized box nails

Folding Trellis

The folding trellis works like an accordion, so its height and width can be adjusted for various situations. The critical phase of the construction is the spacing of the pivot holes. These must be accurate on each piece for the trellis to open and close smoothly. Do a careful layout on one piece and use it as a pattern to drill others individually or by stacking them. The slot in the end posts is necessary so the terminal points on the trellis can move freely when you are making a size adjustment.

The concept permits the use of any size of material. You can, for example, work with ¾-inch stock if you need more rigidity than lath provides. If you do make a change, be sure to purchase cotter pins and carriage bolts that are long enough for the job.

Two folding trellises being used for a row of tomatoes

How To Determine Dimensions

A = width of material
(standard lath = 1½" wide x ¼" thick)
B = ½ (A) C = ½ (A) D = E
F = 6 (D) plus A G = 5 (D) plus A
H = 3 (D) plus A I = D plus A
Sample trellis shown here has pivot holes 8" O.C. and requires

F =	8 pcs.	1¼" x ¼" x 49½"
G =	4 pcs.	1¼" x ¼" x 41½"
H =	4 pcs.	1¼" x ¼" x 25½"
I =	4 pcs.	1¼" x ¼" x 9½"

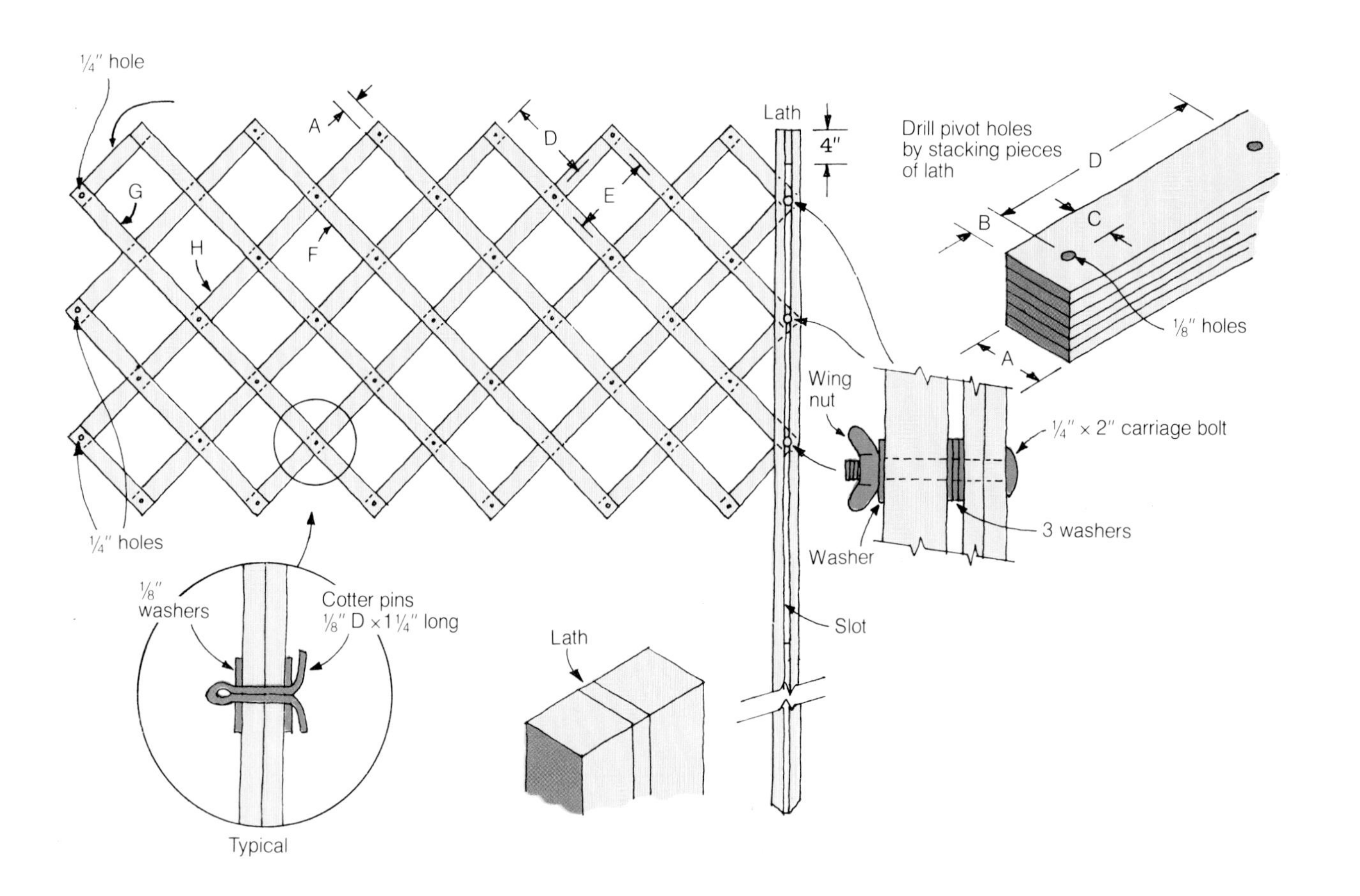

Interwoven Trellis and Portable Posts

These trellises can be used individually, or combined as screens for wide areas, or to provide espalier support for lines of plants in pots or in the ground. They can be moved anywhere when mounted on portable posts.

You can make the grooved frames with standard materials. Or, you can take $1\frac{1}{2} \times 2\frac{1}{2}$-inch stock and run a $\frac{1}{2}$-inch-wide by 1-inch-deep groove down the center of it with a table saw. Don't make the grooves narrower because you'll need the width when you weave the lath or overlay the strips—whichever you decide to do.

The best procedure is to assemble three sides of the frame, install the lath, and add the fourth frame piece. Lath is easier to weave if you soak it first. Plan for openings 6 to 10 inches square. Woven strips will be tight enough so you won't need fasteners where they cross or end in grooves. Overlaid strips need a nail at each crossing point.

The portable posts are 2×4s imbedded in concrete in 10-inch clay pots. Remove the bottom of pot by using a carbide-tipped blade in a saber saw or with a tungsten-carbide rasp. Drive a few 16d nails part way into the 2×4 to serve as wood-to-concrete anchors. Do the job on level ground and brace posts in true vertical position until concrete sets.

Attach the trellises to the posts with carriage bolts and wing nuts. If you make the posts longer than you need for the immediate application you will be able to raise or lower the trellis at will merely by drilling new holes for the carriage bolts.

Interwoven lath panels and portable posts in clay pots. See page 107 for a photograph of a hide-a-can panel for the bottom.

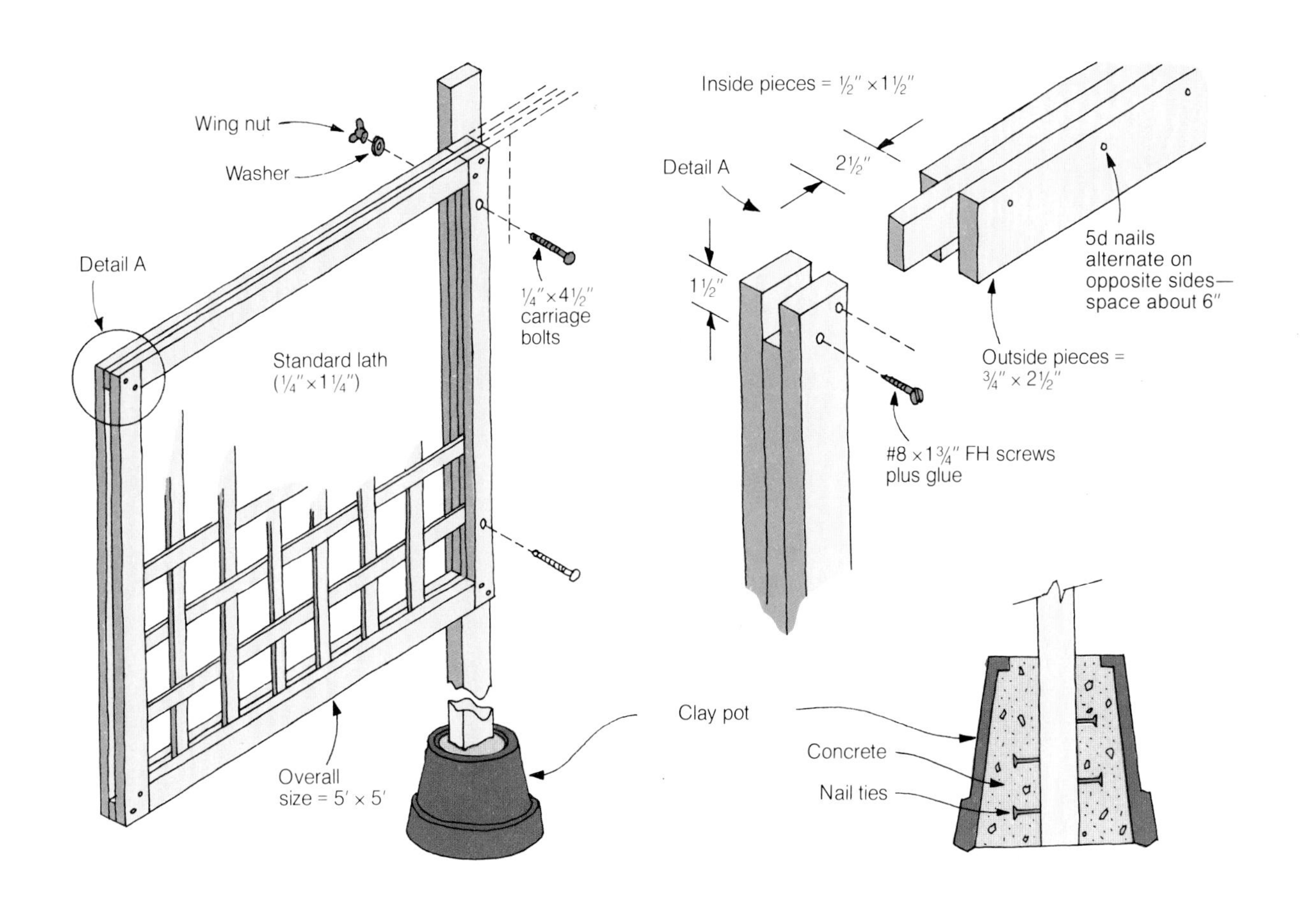

This grape trellis was based on those designed for commercial growers.

The box is the same, but the trellis changes to make this container perfect for espaliering an apple tree. See page 93.

Grape Box

The box for our grape-espalier project is basically the same as the Apple box (above, right) but employs an unusual trellis design very good for grapes. The main difference is the depth of the box and thickness of materials. Here, we work with a 2-inch *surfaced* stock, which nets at 1½ inches, as opposed to the full 2 inches of *unsurfaced* stock used for the Apple box.

Follow the box-assembly procedure for the Apple box—then cut the two vertical and four crossarm pieces for the trellis. Attach crossarms to verticals and then hold assembled pieces in place while you drill holes for the carriage bolts.

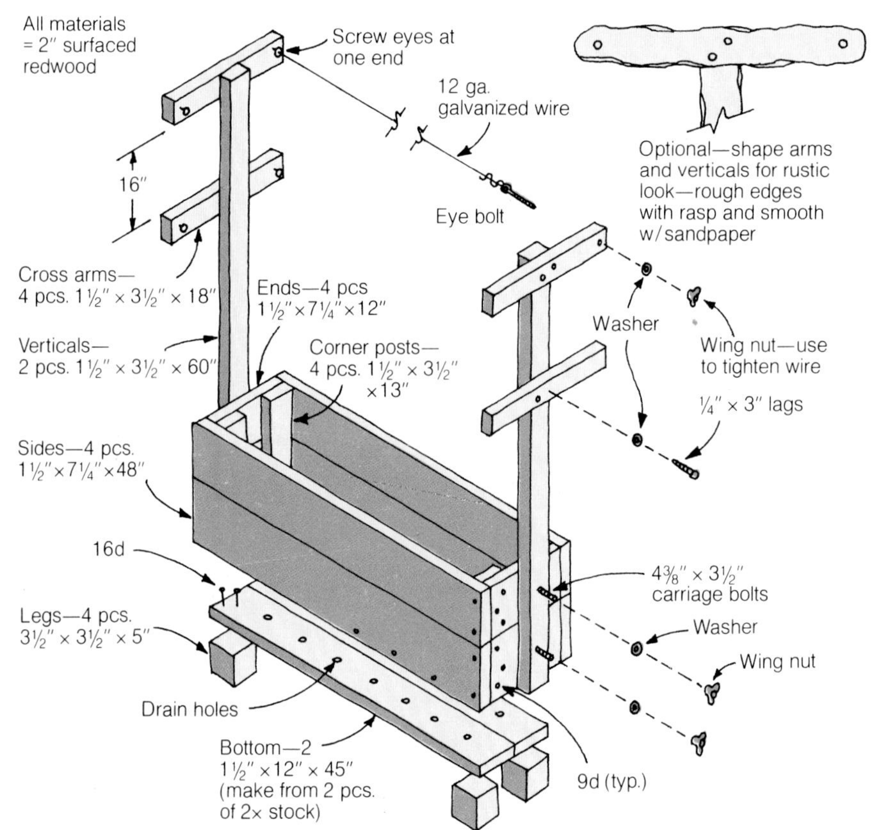

Tomato Box

Before constructing this project, check the drawing and see how the verticals of the trellis are designed as part of the box. Cut all side pieces to length and assemble them to the cleats, but provide for two things—an opening on the back panel so the center trellis-vertical will fit in; and space below bottom cleats so the ¾"-inch plywood bottom can be inset.

Next step is to cut all parts for the trellis. Cut the notches by working with a dado assembly on a table saw or cut and chisel by hand. Assemble the trellis by driving the screws called for at each crossing.

Attach the front panel to the front corners, add the side panels, and then the back panel *and* trellis. In each case, three screws are used on adjacent sides of each corner. Secure the center trellis-vertical by nailing through the back cleats.

Size the bottom and drill through it for drain holes. Place the project flat, on the trellis, and attach the bottom by driving nails along its perimeter into all bottom cleats.

The center vertical on this trellis is optional. Here it's shown both ways.

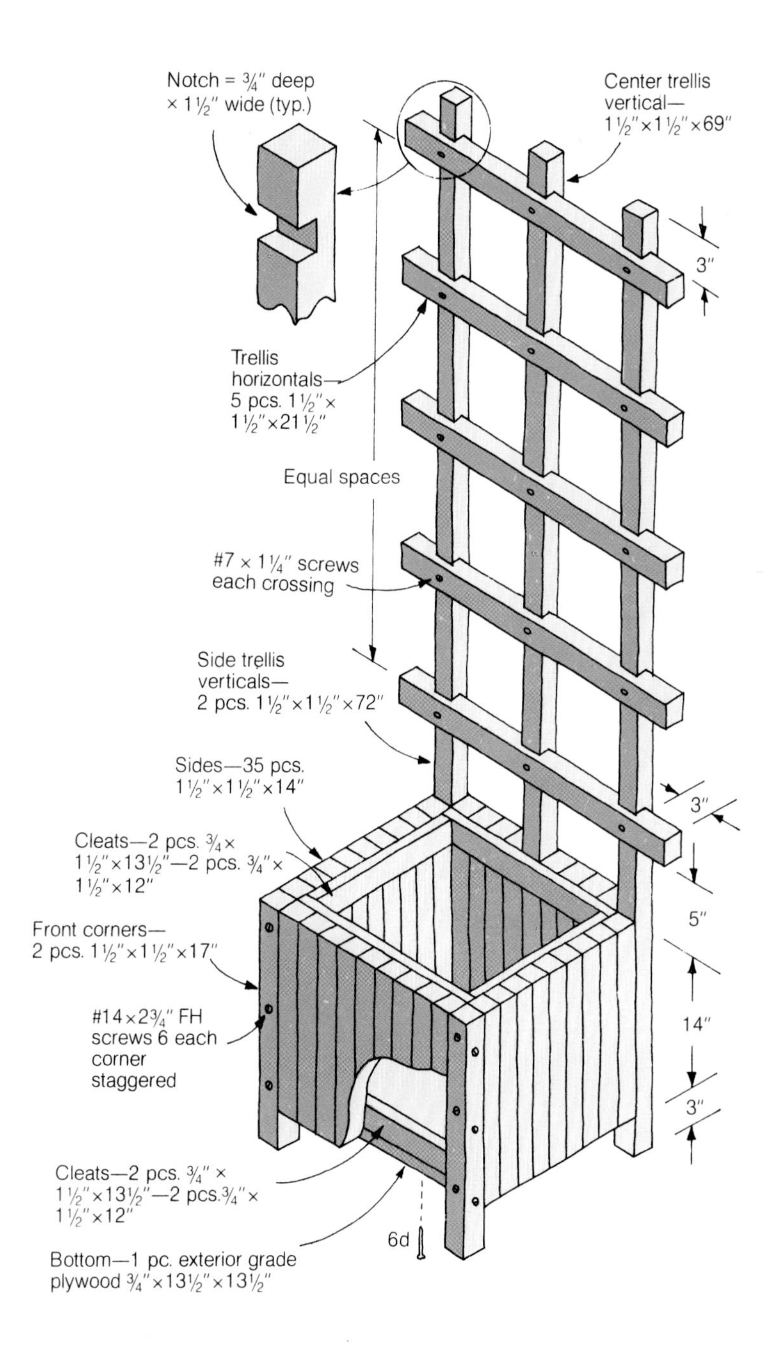

The basic shape of the container is carried through by the trellis for this box. Here it is being used for grapes.

Vine-Crop Box

This handsome container with sloping sides offers the opportunity to use your sawing skills to cut compound-angle joints correctly (requires power cutoff saw). Each corner combines a miter and a bevel—not as simple as a butt or plain miter, but easy enough with a portable electric saw and a miter box.

Place two pieces of 2×12 stock edge-to-edge. Mark two points 30 inches apart on the top edge and a center mark at 15″ on the bottom edge. Now, mark one point at 9″ to the left of the center mark on the bottom and another 9″ to the right. Draw lines from 30″ marks to marks on bottom. Tilt saw to setting of 41¾° and make cuts on lines. This gives you the two pieces for one side of the box. Use these as patterns for other sides.

Nail corner posts into position on Sides "A" & "B." Form box by assembling with "C" & "D." Use box as pattern for bottom. Attach feet before you put bottom in place.

Put the trellis together by attaching the vertical 2×4s first, then the horizontal 1×3s. The latter nailing chores will be easier if you place the project on its side on a hard surface.

Provide drain holes. Seal or preserve the wood if necessary.

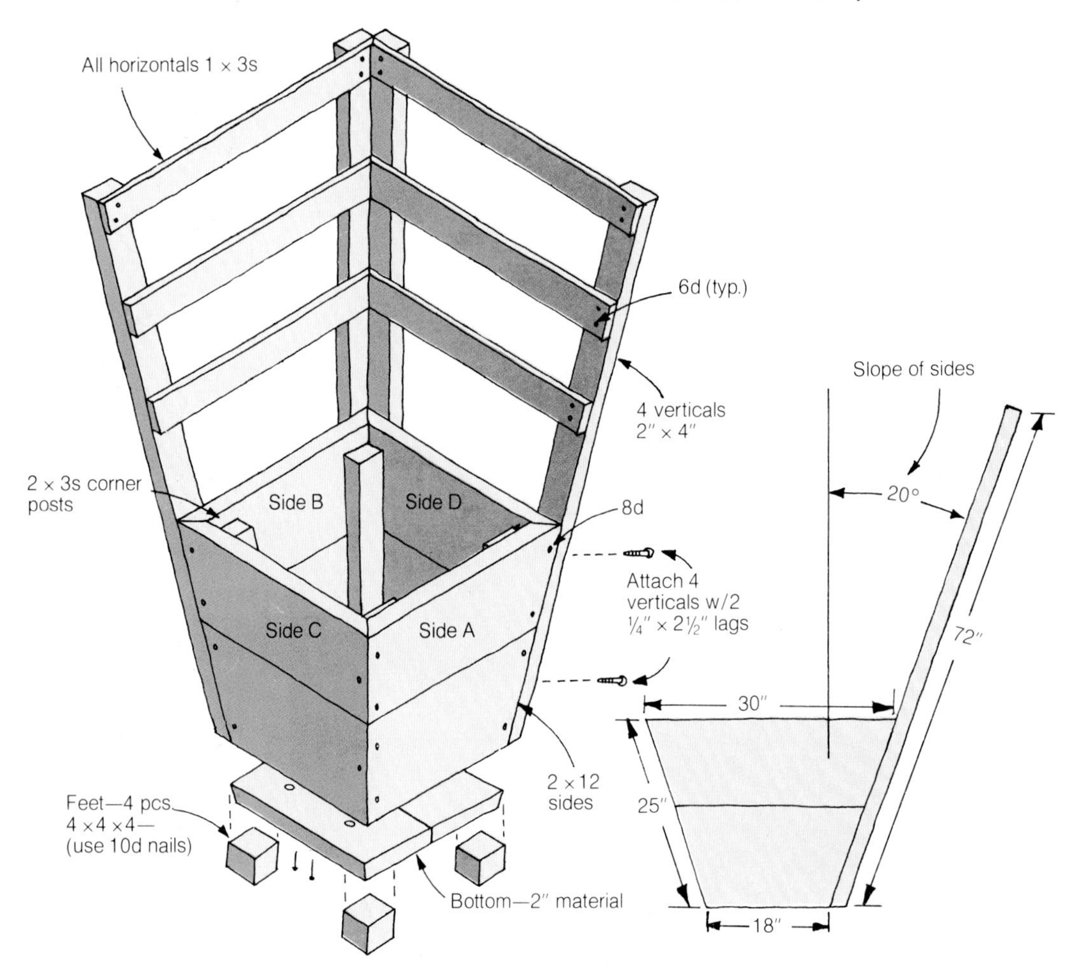

Hide-a-Can Boxes

Many large plants from the nursery will grow for months or years in the containers they come in. If you are not content to look at the nursery container, but don't want to transplant it immediately, we suggest the hide-a-can box.

Made of lath, it is economical and surprisingly good looking. The cover of the box allows the plant container to serve as a low table—a convenient resting place for empty glasses.

Study the drawing and the chart carefully before you cut material for the hide-a-can box. The best procedure is to assemble the sides of the box (lath pieces to body cleats) as separate units and then put them together by driving the 8d nails at each corner. Attach the end lath pieces last, since they may require trimming to fit.

Assemble the lid after the body is finished so you can check its overall size directly on the box. The center opening may be square or round. If square, cut two or three of the middle pieces shorter than the others before nailing to the lid cleats. It's better to cut a round opening after assembly. In either case, saw the lid in half as the last step.

A variation on the box idea using a moveable front panel to hide the cans.

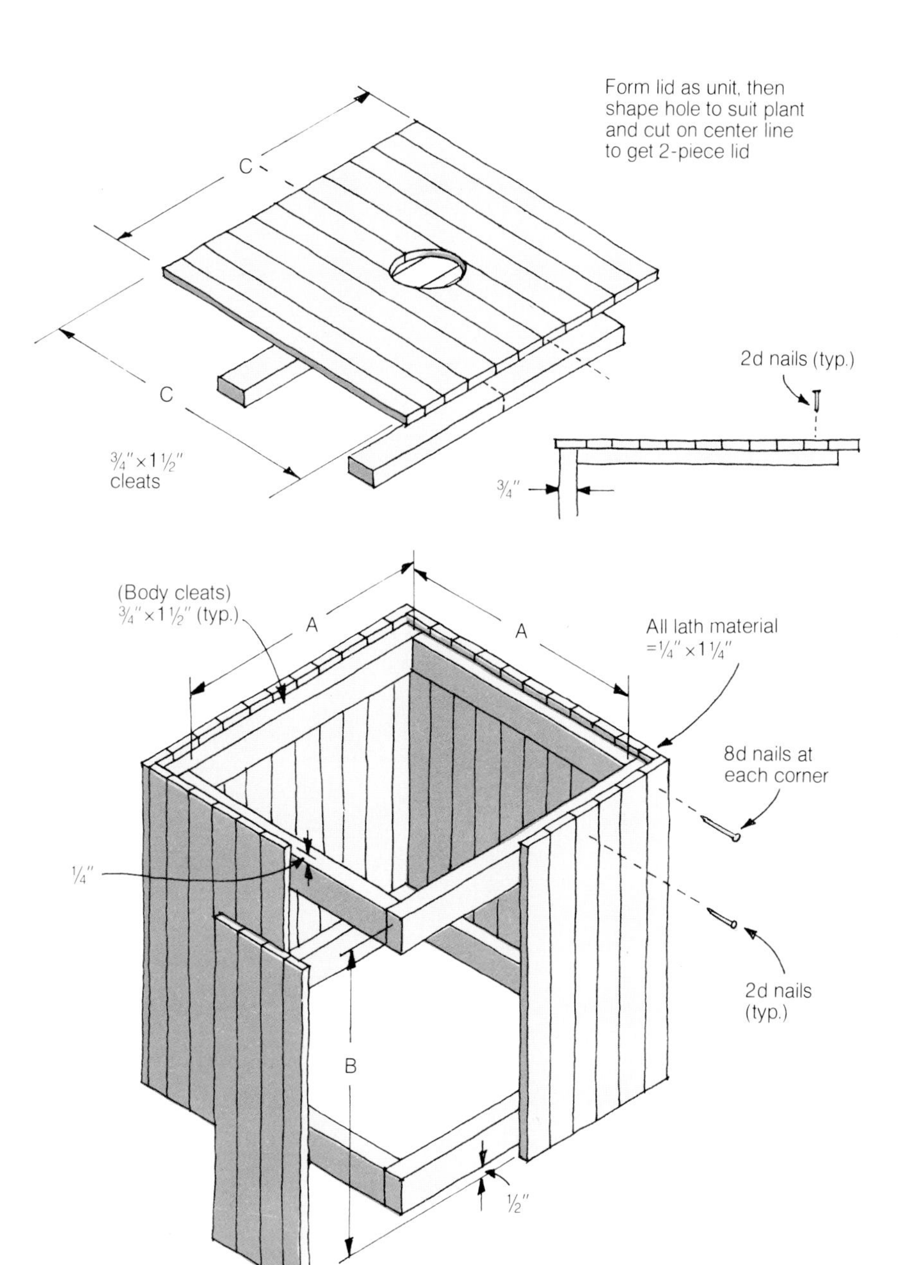

How to determine dimensions

Size of Can	A=	B=
1-gallon	7"	8¾"
2-gallon	9"	9¾"
5-gallon	12"	13¾"
15-gallon	15½"	19¼"

Dimension "B" includes ¾" for the lid cleats on "C". In all cases, "C" = "A" plus 1½"

Index

Page numbers in italics indicate illustrations.